TRUE LEADERS

How Exceptional CEOS and Presidents Make a Difference by Building People and Profits

Bette Price

George Ritcheske

Dearborn™
Trade Publishing

A **Kaplan Professional** Company

This publication is designed to provide accurate and authoritative information in regard to the subject matter covered. It is sold with the understanding that the publisher is not engaged in rendering legal, accounting, or other professional service. If legal advice or other expert assistance is required, the services of a competent professional should be sought.

Vice President and Publisher: Cynthia A. Zigmund
Editorial Director: Donald J. Hull
Acquisitions Editor: Mary B. Good
Senior Project Editor: Trey Thoelcke
Interior Design: Lucy Jenkins
Cover Design: design literate, inc.
Typesetting: the dotted i

Printed in the United States of America

01   02   03   10   9   8   7   6   5   4   3   2   1

Library of Congress Cataloging-in-Publication Data

Price, Bette.
    True leaders : how exceptional CEOs and presidents make a difference by building people and profits / Bette Price, George Ritcheske.
        p.   cm.
    Includes index.
    ISBN 0-7931-4826-X (6x9 hbk)
    1. Executive ability   2. Leadership.   3. Chief executive officers.
I. Ritcheske, George.   II. Title.
HD38.2 .P75 2001
658.4'092—dc21

                                                                2001003648

This book is dedicated to the nonprofit organization, Students In Free Enterprise, SIFE, for the wonderful work they do to develop true leaders and to inspire worldwide the spirit of free enterprise.

CONTENTS

PREFACE

T*rue Leaders* is a blueprint for success in an era when a rapidly changing marketplace and an ever changing workforce require integrating human value with economic value to differentiate effective leaders from ineffective leaders. The ideas and concepts brought forth in this book meet a critical need when the business world is responding to a pendulum shift. Profits alone are no longer the sole measure of success, leaders are seeking significance in their lives as well as financial success, and integrating human interactions with technological innovations to effectively lead change and sustain momentum in future innovations is becoming imperative.

From interviews with nearly 30 CEOs and presidents, you will learn principles that are fundamentally imperative to meet the leadership needs of a new era in which companies face a shrinking workforce and a limited pool of highly skilled employees. Rather than using money as a sole motivation for staying, employees also expect to be valued for their unique contributions, and they want to work in environments where leadership demonstrates that people are not just a commodity needed to get the job done.

Unlike many leadership books based on one specific leader's concepts or an academic approach to leadership, this book draws from a diverse group of leaders within a diverse group of industries: some held publicly and some privately; some led by men, some by women, and some by minorities. We have also included a few nonprofits as well as an elite branch of the United States Government. Leaders interviewed are not profiled. Rather, their wisdom and examples of important leadership characteristics are woven throughout the book so you can learn specifics from them and adapt concepts to your own leadership situation.

True Leaders was born from a conversation we had about leaders who, by reputation, value people as well as profits. As consultants who work with leadership issues at both private and publicly held companies, we saw firsthand the damage an organization's leader can do when focused solely on the bottom line, failing to demonstrate a genuine interest in valuing and developing the very people necessary to generate profits. We saw confusion, distrust, fear, even apathy in midlevel leaders who were desperately trying to read between the lines of unclear communications from those at the top. And we saw others who worried only about salvaging their own careers or beginning to look for new jobs.

During the same period, we observed Americans beginning to examine more consciously what they expected of their political leaders, and we watched economic trust erode as the stock market slowed and the dot-com bubble burst. We watched some leaders rely on lucrative compensation packages to attract talent with get-rich-quick promises rather than using realistic hiring practices.

Yet, in the midst of all this chaos, we also saw companies pull their troops together to forge onward, grow, and even thrive. We saw teams committed to sticking together in difficult times because they rallied to a leader whom they admired, respected, and believed in—even when the leader made tough decisions. What did these men and women at the top do differently, we wondered? What characteristics enabled them to lead an organization where people believed that they were valued and were willing to do whatever it took to get the job done, willing to push harder during tough times, and willing to understand and accept that some of the difficult decisions at the top might eventually cause them to lose their own jobs?

We decided that the only way to find out how these leaders think, and what motivates them to lead with such loyalty and trust, was to go directly to the source. So we set out to talk to the individual who consciously, day-to-day determines the culture, philosophy, and direction of the company—the CEO or President. Now that was a gutsy task for a couple of consultants who were not well known in CEO circles. Yet we believed that if we could identify a core group of leaders who matched our description of true leaders, they would identify with our book concept. We believed that not only would they be willing to be interviewed, but that many would also be willing to help introduce us to other leaders who were of like mind. With that belief firmly in mind, we drew up a list of characteristics we thought would be required of this exceptional kind of leader. We then drafted a fact sheet, providing a brief description of the book's concept and what we hoped to accomplish, short bios of ourselves, and what we were requesting in the way of time and information from each leader. We created a ranking sheet from the ten identified characteristics and asked for their input on any with which they disagreed, and to add anything important that was missing. We also asked them to complete a one-page assessment called the Personal Interests, Attitudes, and Values instrument developed by TTI Performance Systems, so that we could validate the primary values that drive their motivations.

We wanted the CEOs and presidents to be representative of a cross-section of companies; not just highly recognizable name corporations, but lesser known, successful entrepreneurial and privately held firms as well as a few nonprofits. We wanted a cross-section of America, selecting companies located from coast to coast. What we didn't anticipate was that we'd eventually be led to an exemplary leader within a division of the United States Government who is making sweeping changes in a positive way.

We began our list with leaders with whom we had directly worked or those we had some awareness of, having worked within their companies at a management level. We also looked to the *Fortune* list of The 100 Best Companies to Work For and then talked with business associates and colleagues who could help us gain access to leaders of the companies selected. We also asked our interviewees for recommendations.

As we began to talk about this book, we did encounter a few naysayers, who told us we had to be crazy to think that we could meet with busy CEOs. But we held firm to our belief that the true leaders from whom we wanted information would want to contribute their thinking and experiences so others could benefit. We were right.

Most of our initial contacts accepted quickly. Some were amazingly quick. Jack Lowe, CEO of TD Industries, answered his own phone and scheduled an interview by the end of the call. David Walker, the Comptroller General of the United States responded via e-mail in four days telling us whom to call to schedule the time. Ann Hambly, Managing Director of Prudential Asset Resources, responded to our voice mail the very same evening, calling from her hotel room while on a business trip to Newark, New Jersey. Len Roberts, Chairman and CEO of Radio Shack, was so cooperative that on the same day we met him and asked him to participate, he not only agreed to do the interview, but completed and faxed back the assessment and ranking sheet within hours. Jack Kahl, the founder of Manco, Inc., offered to make it easy for us by meeting with him in Dallas while he was in town to attend a board meeting for Students In Free Enterprise (SIFE, an organization we were so impressed with that we decided to dedicate this book to them, along with a percentage of our royalties). He also urged us to interview SIFE's CEO, who in turn invited us to attend the organization's Board dinner so we could meet additional CEOs. Not only did these leaders embrace what we were trying to do, they reached out in incredible ways to help us do it better.

If you think these CEOs and presidents responded because of ego—that they liked the idea of being written about in a book—you are wrong. Yes, they have an element of ego, as one would expect from most people who ascend to the top. However, we found their egos to be very much in check. In fact, most of these men and women demonstrated a very unique mixture of power, confidence, and humility. Several confessed to giving interviews rarely but noted that our concept hit a chord with them. We believe their responses came from one consistent thread—a genuine passion for people, a desire to help others, and a feeling that their leadership made a difference beyond generating company profits.

In our early search, we did encounter a few presidents and CEOs who on the surface appeared to be someone we'd like to include. It didn't take long to know that they did not fit our profile. In some instances, their peers candidly told us, "I don't think so." In other instances, actions warned us that the individual might not really measure up to the standards of those we were seeking. The red flags came in one of two ways—from the process of trying to reach the leader, or from the tone of their initial response. For example, one CEO who had been touted as operating with a totally open style was shielded by a myriad of gatekeepers the likes of which we had not experienced with any of her counterparts. To this day, we are not sure whether the request ever got to her. Yet the fact that she had built so many layers within the organization to impede access speaks loudly when compared to the processes put in place by her peers.

Another CEO, whose company landed on the *Fortune* list, caused us to think he might not be doing the interview for the right reasons. He had his executive assistant call back to find answers to a litany of questions, many of which seemed to us rather self-serving. Questions like: How many bookstores will carry your book? How many books will actually be sold? Suffice it to say, we did not continue pursuit of this individual. Fortunately, these situations were rare, and you will not find these individuals in this book because their actions truly spoke louder than words.

There are undoubtedly other leaders you will not find in this book who should have been included. Time became the determining factor. Even now, in our final stages of completing this book, we are encountering other exceptional CEOs and presidents who would have, had we had more time, been ideal to include. We believe their thoughts and ideas would closely mirror the exceptional leaders who *are* included in the book. They are the kind of leaders who we believe have stayed the course of true leadership while others have strayed afar or simply were never on a similar path.

Dan Woodward, who spent his early leadership development years at IBM and is now Chairman and CEO of Enherent Corp., described well how many leaders have turned from the basic foundations of true leadership. "All of this chaos has caused business to take its eye off the most important ingredient," Woodward said. "Too many leaders today don't develop their people. They've stopped investing in them. They're focused on technical core competencies only. I think one of these days we're going to pay the price for it."

We believe many of these companies are already paying the price in the form of high employee turnover and lack of loyalty and commitment. James Copeland, Jr., CEO of Deloitte & Touche, makes no bones about the importance of people. "Here," he says, gesturing to indicate the firm's New York office space, "we've got nothing but a few desks and chairs and $12 billion worth of annual value created through the minds of the intellect of our people. People are not just one of the firm's greatest assets, they are our ONLY asset."

The truth is, people are *your* only competitive asset, too. Yet far too many companies have been so consumed with the race to accelerate economic growth, that some of the basic leadership principles so critical for sustained growth have been ignored. There is another way. Perhaps you will see this book as a wake up call. Whatever your leadership stage may be, you can learn much from these true leaders. As you discover the principles of these leaders, you will begin to see that some of what sets them apart from leaders in general is that they are balanced in their thinking and motives, they have common values that drive their decisions, they truly care about the people they lead, they are passionate about their company and its purpose and express their feelings openly, they have a balanced view of profit making, they aren't embarrassed to show their sensitivity, and they darn well believe you'd better tell the truth—particularly in difficult times.

As you move through the pages of this book, you will read some great firsthand examples of true leadership, and you will enjoy the rare opportunity to get inside the heads of some exceptional men and women who share candidly their personal wisdoms and strategies for leading with passion and purpose. Whether you are an aspiring leader or already in a leadership position, and whether you are in a large corporation, a small or privately held entity, or a nonprofit organization, you can learn much here. *Explore and Discover* questions at the end of each chapter provide self-discovery opportunities to help you explore your own leadership development.

As Jack Kahl says, "The first highway to developing yourself starts with reading about another successful person." Here you have nearly 30 successful people to read about and learn from. Enjoy the learning! Commit to the doing! And apply it in your own style!

The true leaders you are about to meet have been insightful, candid, inspiring, and incredibly willing to share their beliefs and their wisdom because they believe in the development of true leaders. Through their sharing, they hope to make a positive difference in your leadership development. In alphabetical order, here are our true leaders:

- Garrett Boone, Chairman and Cofounder, The Container Store
- Terri Bowersock, Founder, Terri's Consign and Design Furnishings, Terri's Consign and Design Franchise
- John Bruck, Chairman and President, BHE Environmental, Inc.
- James Copeland, Jr., CEO, Deloitte & Touche/Deloitte Touche Tohmatsu
- Debbie Gaby, President, Sleep America
- Len Gaby, CEO, Sleep America
- Ann Hambly, Managing Director, Prudential Asset Resources
- Frank Hennessey, CEO, MascoTech
- Vicki Henry, CEO, Feedback Plus, Inc.
- Irv Hockaday, President and CEO, Hallmark Cards
- Linda Huett, President and CEO, Weight Watchers International, Inc.
- Jack Kahl, Founder, Manco, Inc.
- Jack Lowe, CEO, TDIndustries
- Bill Matthews, Managing Partner, Plante & Moran, LLP
- Mike McCarthy, Chairman, McCarthy Building Companies, Inc.
- Gary McDaniel, CEO, Chateau Communities, Inc.
- Gary Nelon, Chairman and CEO, First Texas Bancorp, Inc.
- James B. Nicholson, President and CEO, PVS Chemicals, Inc.
- David Novak, Chairman and CEO, Tricon Global Restaurants, Inc.
- Dr. Alvin Rohrs, CEO, Students In Free Enterprise
- Len Roberts, Chairman and CEO, Radio Shack Corporation

- Bruce Simpson, CEO, AppGenesys, Inc.
- Lou Smith, President and CEO, Ewing Marion Kauffman Foundation
- Kip Tindell, President and CEO and Cofounder, The Container Store
- David Walker, Comptroller General of the United States, U.S. General Accounting Office
- Tim Webster, President and CEO, American Italian Pasta Co.
- Dan Woodward, Chairman and CEO, Enherent Corp.

ACKNOWLEDGMENTS

This book was written with the help and encouragement of many people. First we offer special thanks to our immediate families:

John Price; Mary Margaret Price; Larry Holt; Lani, Robert, Brittany, and Lauren Calbert; Blake, Darlene, Austin, and Alexis Lind; and Bobbi, John, and Katie Ritcheske.

We thank all those who granted interviews and gave generously of their time. They are listed individually in the preface section. We also give thanks to our special friends and associates in the National Speakers Association who helped us in their own individual ways: Lisa Aldisert, Ben Brown, Patsy Bynum, Tim Durkin, Barbara Glanz, Mark Holmes, T. Scott and Melanie Gross, Linda Hanson, Elizabeth Jefferies, Clare Rice, and David Rich.

A huge thank you to Bill Bonstetter and TTI Performance Systems for assistance with the accumulated scoring and results of the Personal Interests, Attitudes, and Values assessment, administered to each interviewee.

Friends and business colleagues were there for us in a number of special ways, and to them we give very special thanks: Royce Baker, Bill Bufe, Dimi and John Campbell, Marian Cherry,

Brian Dersken, Steve Doyal, Sharron Driskill, Stephanie Ertel, Dick Grote, Janet Hill, Donna Howell-Sickles, Cheryl Jensen, Chuck May, Debbie McCoy, Charlotte Merrill-Davis, Bernice Bede Osol, Naomi Replogle, Bobbie Ritcheske, Jan and Les Simms, Noreen Whelan, and Dr. F. David Winter.

A special thanks to Jack Kahl for introducing us to the Students In Free Enterprise (SIFE) organization and to Tajna Heinen, Vice President of Development for SIFE, for her coordination and support and for inviting us to participate in their regional and national competitions so we could see firsthand the magnificent work that fosters ethical leadership and free enterprise.

Last, but certainly not least, we thank Dearborn Acquisitions Editor Mary Good for her belief in the project and her constant support and guidance, and vice president and publisher Cynthia Zigmund for her faith and commitment. And, to our entire book team at Dearborn: Elizabeth Bacher, Publicist; Leslie Banks, Publicity Manager; Robin Bermel, Marketing Director; Nakisha Haywood, Public Relations Assistant; Don Hull, Editorial Director; Lucy Jenkins, Art Director; Terri Joseph, Special Sales; Jack Kiburz, Senior Managing Editor; Paul Mallon, Director of Sales; Kay Stanish, Manager of International and Subsidiary Rights; Trey Thoelcke, Senior Project Editor; and Sandy Thomas, Senior Editorial Assistant.

1

True Leaders Defined

True leaders are a rare breed. They stand out from other leaders because of a strong set of core values that motivates and drives them to:

- Genuinely demonstrate an inherent love and caring for people
- Expect results and profits, yet not be consumed by them
- Be competitive when necessary, yet exercise control judiciously
- Operate from a fundamental belief system that guides them in all decision making

How do we know what values motivate the men and women interviewed for this book? Because we profiled each of them using a highly validated instrument called the Personal Interests, Attitudes, and Values assessment, a product of TTI Performance Systems, Ltd., a research-based company that specializes in assessment tools and training programs related to performance improvement issues. The instrument measures six business values and provides a national mean point for each. When we compiled all the reports of the leaders interviewed to determine what the average profile would look like, we found that the attitudes reflected by the average true leader reflect:

- *A strong belief about helping others to achieve.* They genuinely value and care about people, and helping others is their primary motivator. The average true leader is able to relate to people at all levels of the company and to respect each for the contributions that they bring to their individual jobs at their respective levels.
- *A realistic concern for profit and results.* They are not driven by money alone, but they are realistic and driven by practicality. They will evaluate business moves for their utility and economic return and will be willing to work long and hard to achieve desired results.
- *A competitive nature, yet never ruthless.* Each situation will be individually evaluated to determine how much or little power and control will be exercised. Power does not equate total control; rather it is exercised with discretion and balance.
- *A strong desire to control the destiny of other people.* They do not merely focus on controlling their own destiny. They have a system for championing the things they believe in strongly.
- *A hearty resilience.* They accept things without taking them personally and have the resilience to take their hits, pick themselves up, and move forward.

Six business values were measured. The intensity of each determines the extent to which the true leader is motivated or driven. Because the average value ranking was within the national mean, the intensity reflects a very balanced drive in each value. The six values measured include:

1. *Theoretical.* A quest for knowledge and the need to order and systematize knowledge for practical use.
2. *Utilitarian.* A value for money and a return on investment, whether time or money. A measure for practicality and results.
3. *Aesthetic.* A need for beauty, form, and harmony versus the utility of objects. A desire for self-actualization.
4. *Social.* An inherent love of people and a genuine desire to lift and develop the potential in others.
5. *Individualistic.* A desire to have the power to control one's own destiny and influence the destiny of others. A competitiveness that varies by the intensity of the value and the specific situation to determine how much or how little control will be exercised.
6. *Traditional.* Strong beliefs within a system that the individual feels most comfortable with. This system can be found in such things as religion, conservatism, early childhood influences, or any authority that has defined rules, regulations, and principles that the leader has used as a guide for living.

From the onset of this project, we believed that we would likely find different behavioral styles among our interviewees, but that they would likely all possess similar values. We were right. Four values surfaced as the average dominant motivators for true leaders:

1. Social
2. Utilitarian
3. Individualistic
4. Traditional

Aesthetic averaged as the lowest value. We will point out the significance of this later. Social was important to all of them and ranked among the top four values with each individual interviewed. Our premise was that true leaders genuinely care about helping people as much as they care about generating profits. This hypothesis was validated.

We asked Bill Bonstetter, Chairman and CEO of TTI Performance Systems, the distributor of the assessment, to comment on the results of the assessments based on his expertise. Evaluating the collective data, Bonstetter noted that while there is more than one way to the top, these leaders were driven to the top by some very similar attitudes and values. "Here's the thing that these leaders have in common—Social is very important to all of them. Social averaged as the number one value. They really value people. We can see that the thread that is most important is their genuine caring about others, and this is something that came from their hearts, not from their heads. So I'm seeing here a group of people that have a strong belief in helping others. And let's not view Social as giving things away, nor is it truly empathy either. Because Social is really 'I care.' If you've got a choice between yourself and others, the higher Social person will truly put the caring emphasis on others.

"The second thing that jumped out to me is the Traditional value. Traditional tells me, from a leadership standpoint, that they do want to control the destiny of other people. If you are high Traditional, you want to control the destiny of other people. If you are low traditional, you only want to control your own destiny. If you're high Traditional, your belief in your own beliefs is so strong that you will champion your cause—whatever it is." Individually, Bonstetter points out, the strong beliefs and causes may differ. What is common, however, is that each has a strong system for carrying out what they believe in.

As for the Individualistic value, Bonstetter says, "It has to be carried out in another value because in and of itself, it just stands for power, which is not necessarily good. But these leaders are going to carry it out in their vision of helping others, tied to some type of practical, utility value in this whole equation, and they will have a strong system for carrying out what they believe in, because otherwise they would not have consistency in working with other people. They may be flexible personally, but they put together a system to make sure that as a group, all their people are on the same page.

"The other thing that I saw was the low Aesthetic value. Out of the six worlds that they could have lived in, only two had Aesthetics in their top three. High Aesthetic people are somewhat sensitive about self, and low Aesthetic people are pretty thick skinned. They don't take things as personally as a high Aesthetic person. Here we have leaders who care about people, are not going to take things personally, and have a vision and a system to carry out what they believe in. If you don't take things personally, you live to fight another day. If you take things personally, you're off in a corner because you're hurt. I think one of the characteristics of people who are successful is resiliency. If you take things personally, it's hard for you to be resilient because things can really get you down. This is a really important aspect of leadership.

"I believe these findings to be a total switch from what we would have seen several years ago," Bonstetter points out, noting that several years ago, Social would have been the lowest value. "This is the most significant change—the attitude toward people in the whole process. The model for leadership really has changed. And it's good. You can be nice to people and still be successful. I think that's an important message."

Check Appendix D for more information on TTI Performance Systems, to see the Attitudes and Values graph of the average true leader, and to find out how you can complete your own assessment and see how your attitudes and values compare to the average true leader.

Based on the top four values, following are some examples of how each value drives the actions and decisions of true leaders.

SOCIAL: THE SELFLESS LEADER

True leaders are keenly aware of the power of their position, yet are quick to point out that without genuinely valuing their people, their position of power is limited. "You can get short-term results by coming into the business totally clinically," says Louisville-based Tricon's CEO, David Novak, "but you get long-term results by building sustainability and the capability of your organization." That requires a genuine, inherent caring about people. "I think you really have to love people," says Garrett Boone, Chairman and Cofounder of The Container Store, the company that *Fortune* identified as the number one best company to work for in 1999 and 2000. "You have to have this compassion and passion that comes through in everything you do. And I think if you are just doing it for posturing, people know." Boone's corporate neighbor and long time business friend, Jack Lowe, is CEO of TD Industries, which has been on the *Fortune* top ten list four years in a row. As a result of the company's visibility in the magazine, Lowe says he gets lots of companies whose people want to come and talk to him. "Generally, they fall into two categories," Lowe says. "One is the group who is sincere and wants to learn more about how to make their own company better. I welcome them. The others come with an attitude that in essence says, 'I see your company growing, you're making lots of money, and you're getting lots of recognition. I want that and I'll fake the other stuff. Give me the gimmicks 'cause I want the results, not the process or not the relationships.'" Lowe adamantly responds, "It won't work."

Lowe knows firsthand the power of building a culture where leadership genuinely cares for its people. Several years ago, when his company encountered a real crisis, the employees took a million and a quarter dollars out of their retirement account and put it back in the company. "That's a commitment based on trust," Lowe said with pride.

At Kansas City's Hallmark Cards, President and CEO Irv Hockaday believes that leaders need to create an environment that allows talent and leadership potential to develop, excitement to occur, teams to form, dialogue to go on, and mentoring to happen. While Hallmark doesn't have a formal mentoring plan, it encourages mentoring on an informal basis. "I think the quality of what happens is better [when mentoring is informal], maybe if it doesn't happen quantifiably as much," Hockaday explains. He also encourages an environment where people feel comfortable taking risks. To demonstrate, Hockaday tells employees a story about the great baseball player, Ted Williams. "In 1941, he [Ted Williams] was batting .401, which is a very high batting average. It was the last day of the baseball season, and it was a double header. The manager of this team said, 'Look, you want to finish this season over .400, because if you do, it will be a record and it will never be broken. So why don't I not have you play in these two games and that way you can't jeopardize your average?' Williams responded, 'Why would I do that? I know how to hit.' He played, he got five hits and ended up with an average of .406, which has never been broken in 60 years."

Hockaday tells this story to impress upon people not to play it safe; that while it is important to know what you're doing, it's also important to take some risks because they are required to help move a company into its future success. "It may sound trite," Hockaday confesses, "but an environment that is caring goes a long way."

Before Linda Huett became President and CEO of Weight Watchers International, she worked for a manager at another East Coast company whom she describes as "one of the most analytical, clinical, and inhumane managers I have ever encountered." While she learned business analysis and strategic planning from him, she more importantly learned that, "if you don't actually have any humanity and any caring for the people that have to get things done, then you're not going to be successful." Huett said she came from a slightly different view. "I felt that if you involved them [people] in the why's and the wherefore of what you wanted them to do, that they would maybe do it in a slightly better way. More importantly, if you [would] go back at the end and praise them occasionally, that you would have better people working for you."

Gary Nelon, Chairman and CEO of First Texas Bancorp, is absolutely convinced that if you are going to do big things, it's the people around you who are going to accomplish it. "You may have the idea, you may have the vision, but without the people, it won't get done. Life is just too short to think of anybody as a commodity or as a tool for accomplishing anything. It is the epitome of short-term focus of doing things." Nelon says that sometimes short-term results are exactly that—they last for a very short time. A favorite expression sums up Nelon's philosophy: "Fast birds don't fly far," he quotes. "You've got to have a perspective that it's more than a short journey, and people are not disposable in that journey."

When Len Roberts took over as Chairman and CEO at Radio Shack, his predecessor told him to take only five minutes when he made his first speech to the organization, because they would be in shock that the company had hired someone from the fast food industry to head up a technology-oriented retailer. Roberts chose not to comply. "I'm not going to take five minutes. I'm not going to waste a moment. We're going to make this worthwhile," Roberts said. It was important to him to take the time to set a new tone so everyone would know how important he felt people were to the new CEO. "I said, people worry about what the change is going to be in this organization. I don't know," Roberts confessed. "I don't know if it's going to be a single change or no one's going to be in this room next year. But I am going to surround myself with people who care and can be trusted." Roberts ended his speech by telling everyone to go to their offices and to find their job descriptions. "Tear it up," he told them, "because from this day forward, there are only going to be two jobs in this company. You either serve the customer directly, or you serve someone who does." It was profound, Roberts recalled. "I actually got a standing ovation."

True leaders have an inherent love and caring for people, and they prove it every day through their principles, their decisions, and their actions.

UTILITARIAN: PRACTICALITY MAKES SENSE

True leaders give freely of their time and resources, but they expect to see a return on their investment. Money is more a yardstick for measuring work effort than for accumulation. They believe hard work pays dividends and are committed to achieving goals. Decisions are usually very practical, evaluated for their utility and economic return. When the value is combined with a strong Social value, they generally give people the benefit of the doubt until practical common sense proves otherwise.

At Chateau Communities, practical thinking led CEO Gary McDaniel to determine that his enterprise needed to move in a new direction to grow the business. "We were bumping up against ceilings, and we had to figure out other ways in order to generate revenue," McDaniel explained. In forging new ground, McDaniel not only wanted the new direction to be successful and profitable but as he says, "more than anything else, I wanted to energize the company to do something different, to take a new direction and to try some new creative things at all levels." It's working, but it took nearly a year for McDaniel to influence general buy-in on the new business development activity—it took methodical, practical, persistent planning that involved the whole team.

When Ann Hambly was hired by Prudential to head up its Asset Resource group, the company had been operating with five locations and five systems. That didn't seem very practical to Hambly. "They hired me, not knowing what I was going to do," she said. Through her analysis, she made a practical decision. "I determined in my opinion the best thing to do was to have one location." For various reasons, she chose Dallas, Texas. The decision was based on practicality, but her strong Social value determined how she would implement the consolidation. "I had to come up with how to do it in the most humane way, without affecting a lot of people's lives, and in the most orderly fashion. The last thing I wanted to do was rip up people's lives and move them, so I had to do it in such a way that was best for the people and the business." Although it was a tough decision, Hambly says even the people who decided to leave the company and take a package were supportive and cooperative.

"I think many times I see in companies a great vision that is sound and wonderful, but no one ever puts it into practical terms and communicates with everyone on how to get it done. So you're not going to get there. I involved all my managers and had them help me every step of the way. I knew clearly what I wanted to have, but I let them reach their own [conclusions] at the same time. What that meant was that I had a manager from each one of those five locations who was on board with this and was a part of the process."

Hambly's handling of a tough decision is a clear example of being motivated by her two top values—Social and Utilitarian.

Mike McCarthy's Social and Utilitarian values are so strong that they totally drove his decision of whether to maximize his return on investment when he retires from McCarthy Building Companies, or whether he'll be happy getting a fair return by putting his people first. "I'm not going to live forever," McCarthy explains. "So I had to decide whether I was going to sell the company to someone outside, which would probably generate more revenue, but would effectively destroy the culture of the company, or sell it to the employees with whom I've had so much fun over the years. This is my family. I worked hard for this company to be the best builder in America, and I've worked real hard to build this family culture. The thought that it would not be there after I leave is anathema, I could not live with it. Money has nothing to do with it. I want them to continue."

True leaders also take a practical view of downturns in the market. "I have always thought that knee-jerk reactions in order to improve stock prices tend to be pretty short term," says Chateau's Gary McDaniel. "The downside about being a public company these days is that it's a very short-term look—everybody's looking at the next quarter's operation, and that's about as far as it gets. They don't necessarily understand the organizational responsibilities. As the CEO of a public company, it is my job to try to balance those things, to deflect that kind of pressure from the organization as best I can, and you try very hard not to make company and organizational decisions based on what the stock price is."

David Novak puts in another way. "You can have a gunslinger reputation for a short bit." However, Novak says, such people don't get a lot of recognition over the long term. From a practical standpoint, Novak acknowledges that there are times that tough decisions must be made. "I've reorganized a lot of companies," he admits. "I've cut a lot of head count and I've fired a lot of people. That's a part of the job, and I will do it again. You can't have your cost structure be fat; it's got to be lean in this environment. You've got to make tough decisions, but that doesn't mean you can't respect people, and that doesn't mean you can't think hard about how to grow the business. I'd much rather grow the heck out of the business; then you don't have those issues."

Make no mistake. True leaders enjoy creating wealth, results, and profitable returns on investment as much as anyone. And when necessary, they make tough decisions. But they tend to put profits into a long-term perspective rather than go for the short-term financial kill.

INDIVIDUALISTIC: POWER AND
CONTROL USED WITH DISCRETION

True leaders have a desire for power and control; not in the sense of command and control, but in setting direction, philosophy, and strategy. "I think people are either strategic or tactical," explains Jim Copeland. "I'm strategic and always have been; I think of things and problems in strategic terms rather than in tactical terms." He says, referring to the global services provided by Deloitte & Touche, "I am not disturbed by ambiguity; it generally helps a lot in this professional services environment. Here, control is best exercised through the culture and the parameters of the organization rather than a decision-by-decision basis." Copeland is quick to point out that the power inherent in the position should never take you away from the fundamentals that brought you to that position of power. "Don't breathe your own exhaust," he urges. "There are some fundamental things that got you into that position of trust; just stick to those values and don't get seduced by the position, because it is seductive."

For some true leaders, controlling their own destiny came early. When Jack Kahl graduated from John Carroll University in Cleveland, Ohio, he was courted by several companies, many of which talked about moving him around to two or three spots as part of his leadership grooming. "I was raised in this close-knit family and they were all in Cleveland," Kahl recalled. "I didn't want to give them up." So one day Kahl sat down and said to himself, "If I'm any good, I'll be good here [in Cleveland], and if I'm no good, I won't be good anywhere else. So I'm going to find out how good I can be." That decision led Kahl to take a job with a small company so he could prove to himself that he had talent. "That was one of the better leadership choices I made for myself," Kahl admitted, "because it was a bet on me, that if I was going to be successful, it was going to be on my own ability." By taking that job at a small company, Kahl controlled his destiny. He later bought the company, turned it into Manco, and grew it into a multimillion-dollar business—not by command and control, but by a very simple motto of family sharing. "Shared information, shared communications, shared rewards, share, share, share. It's my mother and father's kitchen table talks philosophy," he explained. "My motto for a long, long time has been my family. Whenever I have a question or a doubt about what's right, I just use the family as a reference point—what's the right thing to do? The answer is always there."

The individualistic value also drives some leaders to break away from the pack, do things their own way. Plante & Moran, LLP, another company to make the *Fortune* list of best companies to work for, is the ninth largest CPA firm in the country, with 15 offices. It is headquartered in Southfield, Michigan, not New York City where some of the big five CPA firms operate. "We are fiercely independent and we plan to stay that way," asserts Managing Partner Bill Matthews. Why? "Because we are very dedicated to calling our own shots, to determining our own destiny, and to not taking orders from somebody out of New York."

Bruce Simpson has worked in both large, corporate environments and for smaller, entrepreneurial firms. He prefers the smaller organizations. "I like to be in situations where I can have some amount of influence over the way things are run and don't have to feel like I am a square peg in a round hole," says Simpson, the new CEO of San Jose–based AppGenesys, a certified Internet infrastructure company. "A lot of times, I felt that I didn't fit in the culture of a larger organization because I saw things that we were doing that were so opposed to my own thinking." Simpson says in his large company experiences, he saw a lot of bad practices revolving around people and wanted to be in a position where he could influence positive changes in that regard. Today, he is doing that.

A healthy amount of individualistic drive is needed to step up to the challenges faced by most leaders. But, when you're reporting to Congress, having clearly defined parameters from which you can determine how much control to exercise is imperative. That's the delicate situation David Walker lives with as the Comptroller General of the United States. Walker, who heads up the government's General Accounting Office (GAO) in Washington, D.C., has held the nonpolitical position since November 1998. He established parameters early on. "I'm a principled person," Walker says. "I'm a great believer in core values. There are beliefs that drive what you do, and there are also boundaries that set up the limits of what you are willing to do. At the GAO, I embarked upon a process by which we could gain a consensus. What were the core values that drove this organization that could bind us together and that would end up being a foundation for everything that we do internally and everything we do externally? We came up with three:

1. *Accountability.* Describes what we do.
2. *Integrity.* Describes how we do it.
3. *Reliability.* Describes how we want it to be received."

Walker explains that rallying the organization around a set of core values helps in decision making, both with regard to internal and external matters. And it is the core values, plus the professional standards, that govern the work they do. "We have 535 clients," Walker points out. "One hundred Senators and 435 House members. They're all bright, dedicated, public servants. However, they are all politicians. They all belong to political parties. They all represent certain geographic areas. They all have certain ideologies, and many times they think they have the answer to what they want us to do before we have done the work. So, we need to have something that kind of helps us rise above that and helps us to on one hand, serve our client, and on the other hand, serve the American people." The core values enable Walker to maintain control in an ethical, fair, nonpartisan manner. "It's pretty disarming," he admits. "It really helps to make life a lot simpler and increases our effectiveness and manages our risk."

Dr. Alvin Rohrs may be the strongest example of living fully from an individualistic motivation. As CEO of the nonprofit organization Students In Free Enterprise (SIFE), he lives, breathes, and promotes individual control every day of his life. "I have a strong belief that free enterprise is really the expression of personal freedom in the marketplace," explains Rohrs. "It's not just about business. It's not just about entrepreneurship. It's about individual choices." SIFE, which recruits, motivates, and energizes college students to learn about leadership and free enterprise and then teach other people through community projects, operates on more than 1,000 college campuses worldwide. (Read more about SIFE in Appendix A.) "The reason free enterprise or market economics makes sense for Tajikistan is not only that their economy will be better, but [that] it gives that individual in Tajikistan or downtown Cleveland or Dallas the freedom to choose what they want to do with their life," Rohrs passionately explains.

Rohrs admits that he is highly individualistic. "I really don't like supervision, but I sure like to supervise," he says. "I am constantly learning to pull back on that and say, you know, there's a reason people don't want your thumb on them." Rohrs has learned a formula for measuring control. "Something I have learned in the control component is to learn where the waterline is on the boat. If you give people the latitude to make mistakes that are above the waterline, they can mess up all they want and you can shoot all the holes you want in the boat. You've got to go patch it, but it isn't going to sink. But, if they make the kind of mistake that makes one good hole below the waterline, you're sunk. So, what I've learned is to try to get people to understand where the waterline is."

Perhaps James Nicholson, President and CEO of PVS Chemicals in Detroit, Michigan, puts the power of power into perspective the best. "Leaders that make a difference change the world for the better. You can be a leader like Colin Powell, or you can be a leader like Adolph Hitler. They were both leaders, and both inspired people," he reminds us. "But one did the Lord's work and one did the Devil's."

True leaders know the real meaning of power and control, and they use it discriminately.

TRADITIONAL: A SYSTEM FOR LIVING

True leaders have a strong belief system in which they feel most comfortable. At times, they will evaluate others based on their rules for living, yet most of all they let their consciences guide their important decisions. Their belief systems may be born out of such things as religion, early environmental experiences, or the impact of someone extremely influential in their lives. They may be unbending in some beliefs, yet flexible in others. Yet the beliefs they strongly hold will heavily influence the core decisions.

When Dan Woodward talks about commitment, he reflects incredibly strong traditional values. The Chairman and CEO of Enherent Corporation, an e-solutions, outsourcing, and staffing firm, says, "I think something that most leaders don't ever realize is that they are making a personal commitment when they take on the role [of leadership], and until it hits you that you have a responsibility beyond an accountability, a personal responsibility to the people, to the business, to the customers. Until you get there, I don't think you'll ever be able to do all the things you can do for your constituency."

At age 38, Woodward was thrust into the CEO role of a company that 19 months earlier had been featured as the cover story for *Inc.* magazine. Company founder Doug Mellinger's face graced the cover of the magazine along with a headline that predicted, "The Next Bill Gates." In the months following the article, the company's stock, which had in one month soared from a low of $10 a share to a high of $21.63, crashed to $2. Four months later, the company announced that Dan Woodward, the second-in-command, who had been on the job only one and one-half months, was now the new CEO. Five months later, the November 1999 issue of *Inc.* magazine told a different story in an article entitled, "From IPO to Exile, Tales of a Fallen CEO." Woodward was left to deal with an ongoing shareholder lawsuit, an IRS tax audit, and the fact that the company was almost bankrupt. "It was just incredible," Woodward recalled. Yet, in retrospect, perhaps he was the ideal pick for the job. When we interviewed him, we mentioned his high-ranking Traditional value and asked what he believed in so strongly that he would nearly die for it. Without hesitation he responded, "I try to be flexible, but there are just a few things you just don't compromise on—how we deal with each other; really it's ethics. It goes back to commitment and truth. It's having a system. I won't accept transparency. There's no rationalization or excuse in my mind for a leader to be transparent. If you can't support and accept and implement, then you need to make a personal decision and make a change. Tough times are rather unpleasant, but you have to take personal responsibility for things. You have to be an example. You can't say one thing and do another." Driven to put the company's past behind and restore credibility and integrity, he renamed the company and turned it around in 20 months. "The good news is, it's gone, it's behind us," Woodward said. "We've emerged refreshed, we have a fine business model; committed, talented, passionate people, and a much more connected team of folks, and our customers couldn't be more satisfied with what we do."

Woodward is quick to admit that a strong spiritual sense is part of what guides nearly everything he does, including decisions in the workplace. "I don't think you can turn that on or off," he suggests. "I wouldn't necessarily connect it to any specific spiritual framework, like denomination. It's more of a connection. It's what supports me rather than what dictates what I might say or do or react to. It's more a part of how I do what I do; a strong spiritual conviction."

At Feedback Plus, the executive team begins every morning with a reverent prayer of thanks. CEO, Vicki Henry, makes no secret of her priorities, "God first, then family, and then the business," she says. "I think it should be kept in that order, and every morning we say a prayer when we start our business day. God really blessed this company richly and we pray for continued blessings," she explains. "I feel like this is His company and He's in charge of it, so we have a real heavy responsibility to see what we can do with it." Henry points out that participating in the prayer is optional and never forced on anyone. "There's absolutely no obligation and certainly we won't think any less of you," she says. Yet there is little doubt that Henry's Christian principles are the cornerstone of the company and its service philosophy to their customers.

Notably, many of the leaders we interviewed draw from faith-based backgrounds, whether spiritual or religious, to determine principles by which they define their business philosophies. Kip Tindell, President, CEO, and Cofounder of The Container Store, leads from a philosophical position inspired by the Jesuits. "When I wrote the foundation principles, I traced it back to a silly story," he explained. "I went to Jesuit High School in Dallas, and at the time, the Jesuits were a pretty radical bunch. We spent a lot of time studying philosophy and that sort of stuff, and I kept a little file and called it my philosophy epistle. I put in that file everything I had ever heard that was an earth-shattering, wonderful idea, whether a teacher taught it to me or I thought of it myself. I was extremely selective about what I put in that file."

Ten years into the business, the company opened a Houston store. It was so successful that it produced four to five times what was expected and no one, including the staff, was ready for it. The experience was overwhelming. So Tindell called a meeting at the store manager's house. "I was trying to think of what I could say, how I could inspire them [the store staff] with a cause to operate as a unit in harmony." Tindell recalled. "I turned to that philosophy epistle file and came out with a set of 10 to 12 [philosophies]. They were some of the best philosophies that I'd ever heard of. I don't think you should have one set of philosophies for life and a different set for business. People who think that are not successful in business. And if your people love them [the philosophies] and agree with them as fervently as you do, that is a pretty good culture underpinning right there." What evolved out of Tindell's file are the following six Foundation Principles that are today's guide for everyone's actions at the successful retailer:

1. Fill the other guy's basket to the brim. Making money then becomes an easy proposition.
2. Man in the desert (explained below).
3. One great person equals three good people.
4. Intuition does not come to an unprepared mind.
5. The best selection anywhere plus the best service anywhere plus the best or equal-to-the-best price in our market area.
6. Air of excitement.

The *man in the desert* is a story of a man who crawls through the desert, gasping for water. He arrives at an oasis, where the typical retailer gives him water. But, when the same man goes to The Container Store, their employees say, "Here's some water, and how about some food, too? I see you're wearing a wedding ring. Can we call your family and let them know you're here?" The point of the story is that The Container Store holds the philosophy that it doesn't do any good just to hand the customer a glass of water and assume that is all they need. "You're cheating the customer if you don't offer them the opportunity to buy more," explains Tindell. The thrust of the story, therefore, is that offering food as well as water, or selling more than what the customer asked for, is merely helping the customer get everything needed to solve a problem. It's a philosophy that differentiates The Container Store from its competitors and encourages customer service.

Early childhood experiences influence some true leaders's business principles. Radio Shack Chairman and CEO Len Roberts talks about coming from humble beginnings and being raised in an ethnic Chicago neighborhood at a time of integration. "My father was a civil rights activist," Roberts tells. "We were scorned, we were made fun of, we were beat up in school because of my father's beliefs. You saw hatred and racism. We empathized with the people who really suffered a lot." Early childhood experiences no doubt played an integral role when Roberts stepped into unexpected problems after accepting the CEO position at Shoney's, the fast food chain, in the late 1980s. Roberts said he was aware that Shoney's had gotten deeply into debt when he took the job. What he didn't know was that the fast food company was in the midst of the largest discrimination lawsuit in history. Roberts said he spent half his time retooling the company and the other half trying to settle the lawsuit. In an unusual turn, Roberts suggested that the founder and former chairman of Shoney's do the right thing and pay the bulk of the settlement—about $65 million. The chairman eventually agreed to the terms, Roberts said, but added a caveat—only if Roberts would go. So he did. Shoney stock fell by 30 percent after *The Wall Street Journal* reported "Roberts Resigns," and shortly thereafter, Roberts was offered the top spot at Radio Shack where he continues to operate with an attitude of fairness and inclusiveness, determined to do what's morally right.

Lou Smith is President and CEO of the Ewing Marion Kauffman Foundation in Kansas City, which engages in grant making and operating programs in the areas of youth development and entrepreneurship. Prior to becoming CEO of the nonprofit, he was a president of Allied Signal. He recalled how important it was, as a young engineer, to hold firm to his fundamental beliefs when he was hired by the semiconductor company. "Remember, that in 1966, things were a lot different," he points out, referring to the fact that he is an African American. "For whatever reason," Smith recalled, "I was able to get into an organization in which, as Martin Luther King said, the content of the character, not the color of the skin made the difference. People took me under their wing and made sure I moved around." One memorable moment of incredible support was when one of his primary mentors insisted that he go back to graduate school to get his MBA. "You don't have an MBA," Smith told the man. "He looked at me and did this," Smith said, rubbing his hand to make reference to the fact that he was African American. "Because of the color of your skin, there are those who will look for ways to hold you back. We're going to put so many stars on your résumé that there is not going to be any way they can."

Despite his mentor's support, the incident pointed out the unfair discrimination he would encounter from others. But Smith's foundation had long been laid about how to deal with prejudice. "It starts at home," he explained. "My parents would never let us use color as an excuse. It even evolved into a personal philosophy that if you look for negatives in life, you're going to find them. So don't internalize the negatives so much that they become debilitating. They're there, but, as Henry Ford said, 'Obstacles are those frightening things you see when you take your eye off the goal.' So, until you've done all you can do, don't use that as an excuse."

True leaders draw upon life-changing experiences, religion, and spiritual beliefs to develop a system for living. These different, yet similar, values play an integral role in how they live their lives, both personally and in business. Their combined primary values drive the characteristics that they have determined are critical in their leadership roles.

So, you may ask, are true leaders born or developed?

"True leaders are made, they're not born," says Manco Founder Jack Kahl. "But, I think they've begun to be made in their childhood where your early community, family experiences, and teaching experiences are very powerful." We agree, to the extent that most of the individuals interviewed seemed to have early childhood recollections of incidents that demonstrated natural tendencies to lead. As a result of these interviews, combined with insights from our previous work, we believe that both genetic and environmental factors are at work. Frequently, when asked, "When did you first see yourself as a leader?" interviewees would respond with early childhood memories of an inherent desire of wanting to lead. "That's a good question," Hallmark's CEO, Irv Hockaday, responded when asked if thought leaders were born. "I don't know the answer, but I would guess that occasionally leaders are born, but more often they are developed. I think those who have both the potential and the desire can be developed. I've seen it, so I know it can be done." We believe the potential is the genetically inherent part that is eventually manifested with encouragement from others such as parents, nurturing relatives, teachers, coaches, and eventually workplace associates.

Tim Webster, CEO of American Italian Pasta Co. says he saw himself as a leader very early in his life. "I always wanted to be the leader when it was student government or even in my group of friends, or if we were playing on the sports team," Webster recalled. "I've always had a high degree of ambition. I've always felt I have an ability to assess and formulate a plan, whether it was a play on the playground or in the basketball or football game, I've always had a point of view—ambitious, opinionated, and willing to put myself out there, willing to take risks." Ann Hambly of Prudential Asset Resources says she saw herself as a leader before other people did—more of an inherent trait. "My mom says that when I was five or six, I asked if I could have a birthday party, and she said, 'we'll see—we'll think about it.' Then she started getting phone calls from moms RSVPing to my birthday party and so she said, OK. Apparently I had taken 'we'll see,' as a positive sign to make my own invitations. She was so shocked that I had taken so much initiative to do that, that she let me have the party." Hambly explains that because she had several younger brothers, she became a leader to them—even though they didn't always like it. It's a leadership trait that was recognized and encouraged early in her career as a secretary. "I started out as a secretary and got into loan servicing accidentally, young into my career," Hambly explained. "One boss, one day, did something incredible. I was probably 24 [years old] and he said that he just wanted me to know that he had been an observer of me and I had only worked for the company three to four months and he was very impressed with me. 'I think you are going to go very far in your career,' he told me, 'and I would like to make sure you stay with us as long as possible. So, I'm going to give you an increase.' He gave me about a 40 percent increase. I think he got me to see my potential."

ApGenesys CEO, Bruce Simpson, clearly remembers the eighth grade as being the first time he saw himself as a leader. "I might have been a leader before that, but I first saw myself as a leader then. I was president of my eighth grade class, which was a tremendous learning experience for me. The reason I saw myself as a leader then is that when we had this discussion—there were about twelve of us, pretty small class—our teacher said we needed to get together and elect a president. Everybody said, 'Bruce, Bruce, Bruce.' I was sort of pressed into service, so to speak. And, what dawned on me after that was that whether I wanted to or not, I was kind of a leader of that class because people had put me into that role. It was a very formative piece of my childhood."

As an adult, James Copeland, CEO of Deloitte & Touche, says that it is difficult for him to think of any organization that he was ever a part of that he didn't lead. "I've been fascinated with leadership my entire life," Copeland admits, "and I have finally concluded that the only real constant strain that I see in leaders is that they wanted to lead." Copeland says he has seen people with eminent qualifications for leadership—attractive, intelligent, nice, all the things one would want to see—"and they will lead, but not in the way that you or I would think of as being a particular relevant feature of their accomplishments. It has something to do, I think, with a desire for control. Not control in the sense of managing the details, because no one would ever accuse me of being an underdog or a control freak. But, I am sort of control oriented at the directional strategy level. I really don't like other people setting the direction and strategy of the organization. Now, I'm perfectly willing to have people accomplish that and give them a wide latitude in terms of how they do it. But, at the very top level of strategy, I really want to be the one that is making those decisions."

So, can anyone be developed into a leader—especially a true leader? Probably not. "I don't know that you can really train people to be effective 'people' people," says Gary McDaniel, CEO of Chateau Communities. "I think you can give them the framework. You can send them to seminars, you can talk to them about it, you can send them to management classes, but what really makes people good managers is time and experience and the ability to make a mistake and learn from that. Those that do it become good managers. Those that don't, they don't survive or they're not as good a manager." Self-motivation is the key, McDaniel believes.

Often it takes someone else to point out one's strong leadership skills. PVS Chemicals CEO, Jim Nicholson, says that he was elected president of his seventh grade class. "But, I don't know that I ever saw myself as a leader," he says. "I think the reality is that people sort of select you as a leader. Since then I've led a lot of things, but most of the time someone would come to me and say, 'would you take this responsibility on, would you do this.' I don't go out and say leader for rent. I think you're a leader because people want to follow you, not because you think you're a leader. There's a certain set of circumstances that people say, 'well, somebody's got to lead this, he's the least worst choice. Let's use him.'"

Gary Nelon, Chairman and CEO of First Texas Bancorp, first saw himself as a leader when a former boss had enough faith in him to recommend him to take over a department in the bank. It was a position for which he never expected to be selected. "I was absolutely convinced they were going to do some big search for it [the position], or take somebody who was much more experienced in any number of different aspects of banking," Nelon recalled. "For them to consider me for that job—I guess I started thinking, maybe I've got the ability to do it. Then, over time, it seemed like the work with my church and work with the Ending Landing, where I adopted both of my kids, and United Way of Austin, and other things—it seems like I've wound up in [leadership] positions in those organizations. I've looked at it as an opportunity to give something back. I've truly enjoyed it. If it comes naturally to you and you enjoy doing it, I guess you're supposed to do it. But, going back and thinking about it, that's the first time it ever occurred to me that maybe I could do it [be a leader]." Nelon's conclusion from his own experience is that leaders are developed. "A lot of people think that leaders are born. But, if they're born of their background, they're born of all the things that make them the person that they are. I don't believe that anybody just arrives on the scene as a leader. Some of my greatest feelings of accomplishment are sometimes getting somebody to stretch out of their preconceived notion that they can't do something. All of a sudden they find that with the right amount of encouragement and the right resources, the right tools, that all of a sudden, not only can they [do it], but then they can be the model for others."

Linda Huett, CEO of Weight Watchers International, says that leadership is often difficult to talk about when you're doing it. "It's a lot easier to talk about when you're looking at leaders who work for you," she says. Among her most candid observations about people who do not approach leadership in the best way, is what she calls resume builders. "I think maybe they lose a certain amount of the fun and opportunities that we all have in our work environment because they are not living enough in the here and now," she says. Her advice? "Don't worry about where you're going next. Concentrate very hard on where you are right now. Make the most contribution and the most of your team and the development of where you are right now. The next place will come along. If you're too focused on the next job or the one above that, then chances are you're not going to do as well or as thorough a job on the one you've got right now. I really believe that if you're concentrating on the job right now, then things can open up that you never even imagined or thought of." Leadership, Huett believes, evolves. We believe it evolves when true leaders recognize the inherent leadership characteristics in their people and work to develop those characteristics through encouragement, opportunities, and recognition.

Prior to each interview, we provided each leader with a list of characteristics that we considered important true leader attributes. Each individual ranked the characteristics and gave additional feedback, both on the form and during interviews. From the process, we have identified ten important principles embraced by true leaders. They are not ranked in any specific order because it was quite unanimous among the interviewees that they are all important, playing an integral role in building people *and* profits. In the following chapters we explore these principles, give firsthand examples of how the leaders demonstrate the principles, and provide you with *Explore and Discover* questions to help you think about each principle as it relates to your own true leadership development.

EXPLORE AND DISCOVER

- What role does helping to develop others play in your career?

- On a scale of one to ten, how important is it to you to help others to build their careers?

- Are you driven by results?

- Are you willing to sacrifice others' feelings to achieve your own results?

- Do you need to be in control? To what extent?

- Do you have strong beliefs that you are not willing to relinquish?

- Do you prefer to work alone or be part of a team?

- When you become involved in something that is not consistent with your own value system, how do you react?

- What guiding principles do you use to make your decisions?

- Do people view you as a partner in the process or as a judge of the outcome?

- How do your values measure in comparison to the true leader's?

- What do you do to demonstrate your primary values?

2

PRINCIPLE ONE

Passion Is a Prerequisite

Passion is a prerequisite for true leadership. It provides a compelling reason to stay on purpose, it is the impetus for authentically building an environment that demonstrates genuine love and caring for people, and it ignites the desire to serve a greater cause than profit alone. Len Roberts calls passion "the secret ingredient." The Radio Shack Chairman says, "When you talk about something, you have to be passionate about it so that passion comes through. You have to care. You can't fake caring. You care about the business, you care about the people, you care about them being successful, that's all about passion. If you really understand why leaders fail," Roberts contends, "it's because they are unable to care."

For Hallmark's CEO, Irv Hockaday, passion is essential to a leader's success. "People have to be motivated," he points out. "Some are self-motivated, but in large organizations, they are also motivated through the communications that come their way. In our business, if you're not passionate about the opportunities or the business or the consumer, you're not going to get people motivated. So passion, I think, is a prerequisite to do your job well. I also think it is a condition for getting others to do their jobs well."

As we discussed the issue of passion with these exceptional leaders, we found that they talked about passion from three distinct perspectives: a passion for the business, a passion for the people, and a passion for serving a higher purpose.

A PASSION FOR THE BUSINESS AND ITS PURPOSE

As the founder of Manco, Inc., Jack Kahl is invited to speak to a lot of business groups. The title of one of his favorite speeches is *Don't Park Your Heart at the Curb*. The premise of the speech, Kahl says, is, "Don't leave your heart just for your family, bring it inside and take a risk, because that shows that you're going to show people that you are 100 percent involved in the business and you want them to be 100 percent involved." Kahl says many leaders fail to develop themselves from a human perspective. "That's a very serious thing I'm saying," Kahl emphasizes. "Leaders don't like to share their humanity. Many have a hard time letting their souls out." It's one of the biggest things he sees lacking in leaders. Kahl says too many tend to be afraid to inject their heartfelt emotions into the business so that their people can sense that, "this is a human being, not just a being, not just a bottom-line person." Kahl doesn't understand the fear and points out, "The greatest corporations in the world and the greatest passionate military or spiritual leaders are people that touch your soul, not your head." Kahl believes passion is an issue of the heart as well as anything else. And it's something he often discusses with other leaders because he believes that when the heart isn't there from the leader, the organization becomes vulnerable. He sites as an example a discussion he had with a colleague who owned a $2 billion business. This colleague told Kahl, "It's much easier for me to run a faceless, emotionless company." Kahl said, "The man ran the company with his head, not his heart, and he knew it. They went bankrupt, and I can tell you why. The people feel the coldness and the nonappreciation, so the good people leave, and what you end up with is that there are not enough good people to keep your company together. You end up down there with the dregs and eventually you end up in bankruptcy."

The Container Store is a classic example of a business where the leaders are not afraid to admit passion. "It's built on people really loving to do what they're doing," says Cofounder, Garrett Boone. "As a company, we love the fact that we have a retail concept that allows us to go out and engage with customers and help them solve problems. And the result is, it's very satisfying for us and customers love us. They tell us, they tell their friends, and their friends tell us. You have to have a passion to do that." Boone points out that success takes not only passion from the frontline employees, it also requires passion behind the scenes. He says that one of the reasons that people have not successfully copied his business is because those who try fail to understand the role passion plays in the overall concept. "They look at a retail store and go, 'Oh that's it, you just get products and you get people,'" he says. "Well, that's really hard to do." First, the buying decisions have to be made in the right way so that the stores have a collection of products that are constantly evolving and changing. "Second, the people part is extraordinarily hard," he confesses. It takes a commitment to hire great people and a refusal to compromise the quality of service that the company expects its employees to deliver—an integral part of The Container Store's core philosophies that one great person equals three good people. So they hire only great people! Then, Boone says, one must believe that training really makes a difference and to go forward with that belief by giving everyone the training they need. "You have to have people here to take the very foundation of the passion, which is the fact that we have a company that interacts with our customers and really does something for them." To do that, Boone says you have to have a passion to do all the behind-the-scenes things too. He points to the passion behind the company's annual Elfa sale. Elfa is a brand of shelving and organizational items exclusive to The Container Store. "We spend all year long thinking through the process of that sale to prepare for it," Boone explains. "And the minute we finish, we get a committee of people together to decide what we did well and what we need to improve. So, you have to be passionate about doing it and you have to be passionate about making the process work—inventory control and all the behind-the-scenes stuff that goes with that, because you could have passionate salespeople and great products and nothing ever gets where you need it. The passion just has to be there."

Boone also points out that the company is built upon its employees being so passionate about working for the company that they commit to the role they are doing today as if they are going to do it for the rest of their lives. If a promotion comes along, so be it, but jockeying for the next position is not the way to get there. Where do they find these great, passionate people? Employees. People who already work for the company play a key role by finding and recruiting other great people. Last year 44 percent of all new people hired came from internal recommendations.

What is Garrett Boone's advice to a leader who lacks passion for the business? "Maybe they should do something else."

Passion has played an integral role in establishing American Italian Pasta Company as the largest producer and marketer of dry pasta in North America. President and CEO Tim Webster says, "I think that it is the essence of the ultimate leader's responsibility to create a clearly understood reason for being for the company, and to pursue that reason for being with passion and tenacity." Webster describes himself as more of a passionate, emotive person than cognitive. "I'm motivated by emotion and driven by emotion," he confesses. "I'm fiercely competitive; my greatest joy is winning or doing something well and my greatest fear is losing or failing. I believe that people's motivation will be greater and more sustainable if it comes from the heart and the stomach than purely from an intellectual belief. I think you have to stir them inside." Webster's passionate drive started early. He was 25 years old when he joined the then privately held company as it's Chief Financial Officer. By age 29, he was named president when the company restructured, and a year later became CEO. Five years later, he took the company public and has demonstrated that passion also helps produce profit. The company has continued to sustain its growth since going public, and in 2000, achieved a three-year compounded annual growth rate of 37.7 percent, far surpassing the industry average of 4.4 percent.

Webster says he has found that his passion for the company to be the best for their customers in terms of quality, cost, and service, and his willingness to do whatever it takes within the boundaries of integrity and legal requirements, has probably been the most powerful impact he has had on the employees. "I spend a tremendous amount of time reinforcing the fact that there are only 500 of us in this company. Out of 275 million people in the country, only 500 of them get to work for AIPC." He adds. "Every one of them, every day, influences those three things [quality, cost, and service]. So, I think to rally around in this technologically sophisticated company, the people part around these basic values is the single greatest responsibility I have as a leader of the company."

You won't find passion as part of the curriculum at leading business schools, nor will it even be an elective. Yet in the real world of leading, it plays an integral role. "I got my MBA at the University of Get It Done," jokes Webster. "The business schools of today are sending their people into investment banking and consulting, they are not sending them into a commercial career, which is something I think is a real problem in this country." He points out that when most of these highly educated consultants make a recommendation, they don't necessarily have to live with it. "You can blame the manager for not implementing it. Right? You have no accountability. So ultimately it is in these commercial disciplines [running the business] where you do have to suffer your own decisions." Webster thinks you ought to have to stay in a job long enough that you have to suffer your own decisions. "I don't like the 18-month promotional tracks where all you do is come in, blame it on the guy before, and then go to the next one," he notes. Webster thinks the human element is devalued and minimized by this approach. "We all know that if you're going to make something happen, you better have the people behind you."

Bill Matthews, Managing Partner of Plante & Moran, LLP, which ranked number ten on *Fortune*'s list of best companies to work for, expressed a similar view. "I didn't study at Harvard. I don't have an MBA. But I have a passion for making this place everything it can be," he says. He then makes reference to the firm's Core Purpose, Statement of Principles, and Commitment Statement. "Now, I recognize these are three sheets of paper," he admits, "and there may not be a lot of differences in what they say from what you see in a lot of places. But what we think is the biggest difference is that we work very hard at practicing what is said on these sheets of paper. When we have a challenge like, what is the right thing to do? We say well, what do we say in our Statement of Principles? And we go back to that. We constantly refer to that in making decisions on where we are going. That's why our staff pretty well always knows the decision we are going to make. To us, it is like the Ten Commandments." And, much like life in general, Matthews admits that sometimes a sin is committed. "Our goal is to try," he points out, referring to the firm's Value Statement, which states: *We care. We are guided by the Golden Rule. We strive to be fair.* Matthews admits that from time to time they make mistakes and do the wrong thing. "We don't say we're always fair, but we strive to be fair. We sum it up with a *we care* philosophy," he stresses. "So, if you were around here for very long, you'd be inundated with this culture of principle statements, core values, core purpose, a we-care attitude. We have a very, very strong culture that constantly reminds us of what we are trying to accomplish."

Linda Huett, President and CEO of Weight Watchers International, goes so far as to point out that a passion for the business is what fosters new ideas and growth. "We are an emotional business as well as a product business," she explains. "Our product is emotionally charged in the sense that you can follow a diet, and if it's a sensible diet and it's brought your caloric intake down, you will lose weight. But most of us who have had a weight problem understand that it's not as simple as following a diet. Most of the problems have to do with how we deal with food, how we interact with food, and how we use food in our life, which is often on an emotional level, not an intellectual level." As a result, Huett says that if the leader doesn't have an understanding of all of that, they will look at their product in a very simplistic way. "We don't necessarily make the best decisions, the best choices, the best developments and innovations that we would if we understood the product and passionately believed that we have one of the best solutions in the marketplace." Huett cites the company's successful new Winning Points Program as a perfect example. If only dieticians and nutritionists had designed the program, it would not have been created, she says. Instead, it was designed through a process that involved not only the dieticians and nutritionists, but people from research and marketing, as well as former Weight Watcher members. "Having this interdisciplinary approach is much more laborious and much more time consuming. It is a much more difficult road to development," she admits, but worth it in the long run. "If you didn't have a passion for this process, I think, as a leader of the pack, you would go for a much more simplistic way of doing things, but would end up with an inferior end result."

At PVS Chemicals, Inc., President and CEO James Nicholson is passionate about safety and the integral role it plays in the company's purpose. "The chemical business in not the worst business in the public's perception, it is the second worst business," Nicholson explains. "In other words, tobacco ranks lower than us. So one of the things that I think is very important for the folks who work for this company is that they understand that the public is better off for what we do—significantly better off, they just don't know it." Nicholson explains his passionate position, "You got here by car today," he tells us. "Well, from the microprocessor that helped start it, to the sulfuric acid in the battery that physically started the car, it wouldn't work unless we, or someone like us, did what we do. We make sulfuric acid." He goes on to explain, "The water you're going to drink is not going to kill you. The reason is that we make ferric chloride that cleans water and, therefore, you will not get dysentery from drinking that water. Now are you grateful?" he asks. "Absolutely not! You expect it." Nicholson points out that in some parts of the world, clean water is a luxury. "Those are the kinds of things we do, and people are better off for it, and the folks who work here need to understand. They need to be very proud of what they do."

Nicholson is so passionate about the purpose of the company and its importance that he personally teaches a course that he calls PVS 101. "Every person who works here takes PVS 101," he says. "I teach it three or four times a year, depending on how and when we get a class together. "And there's homework required before it." Nicholson explains that there are eight hours of lectures, games, and role-playing, and at the end, there's a test. "If you don't get 70 percent on the test, you get the joy of spending another eight hours with me. And that's an incredible motivator. If you get 100 percent, you get $100 cash, right there, on the barrelhead, paid by me." Nicholson has made safety the number one core value on its list of nine—known to all employees as the *Nicholson Nine*. If Nicholson catches someone carrying their laminated list of the Nicholson Nine, he gives them $20 on the spot. The absolute number one core value is: Safety is #1. Nicholson tells us, "You can go to anyone in this company and ask them what the number one priority is. If they don't say safety, you have my permission to fire them on the spot because they haven't got the message." Why is Nicholson so passionate about safety? "It's more important than quality. It's more important than customers. It's more important than profit, because we can do something about all of those things, but if safety fails, everything fails." Safety is at the core of PVS's business.

The Chairman of First Texas Bancorp, Gary Nelon, sums up a passionate drive for the business in this way: "If you don't have it, you won't accomplish anything. It takes more than just a desire to want your company to do well. [Passion's] got to be in the back of your mind all of the time. You've got to be living it. You can't just have it as a part-time thought. You've got to have a passion for what the company is all about, and you have to have a passion for the people that are dedicated to those same goals."

PASSION FOR PEOPLE

David Novak thinks leadership is a privilege and right that has to be earned every day. "I don't think leaders should take it for granted that they're a leader," says the Chairman and CEO of Tricon Global Restaurants, which operates three fast food chains—Kentucky Fried Chicken, Pizza Hut, and Taco Bell— worldwide. "A lot of people would like to have my job; I think it is a great job. It's got its demands, but in order to keep a job like this, you have to earn the right to keep it." To make sure his leadership teams around the world understand his philosophy, Novak personally developed and teaches a course to his executives that he has entitled "Taking People with You: Getting Results with Your Team." "My teachable point of view as a leader is, you have to start first with recognizing and building the capabilities of people; it is the most important thing you can do, because nothing gets done in any business unless people make it happen." Novak doesn't understand why some leaders don't get such a simple concept. "If you get people working together, then what happens in our business is that you satisfy more customers. It's amazing how many more customers you can satisfy when people are working together on the right things. Then, when you satisfy more customers, you make more money."

Novak thinks companies get in trouble when they start out thinking about the bottom line versus thinking about how to get there. "You can't get anything done unless you get it done through people," he emphasizes. "When you walk into a restaurant you have to feel the energy from the people. You have to feel the spirit of team. You have to know that they are committed to your satisfaction, and we want that to happen in every one of our restaurants. The only way that happens is if there's a leader in that restaurant that builds a great team and that is motivated to do the right things." That's why, at Tricon, Novak says the restaurant general managers are the number one leaders. "Not me," he says. "I understand that I'm the CEO and people look to me as the final decision maker on strategic issues and all that, but the mindset of our company is that the restaurant general manager is the number one leader because they build the team that satisfies the customers." To make sure this philosophy is embraced worldwide, Novak has taught the program to nearly 600 executives around the world since becoming CEO. "I'm there the whole time, night and day, and I take them through 13 leadership principles that I've learned over time about how to build and align teams. That's been a really powerful thing to do." First, Novak talks about the company, and the things that he has learned and the mistakes he has made. "I'm very vulnerable as far as laying those things out," he admits. Second, over three and one-half days he listens to people from all over the world to find out what's going on in the company from their perspective. "That's been a really terrific thing," he says. Novak says he learned early in his career, which began at PepsiCo, the importance of being passionate about the people in the company.

"When I was in Pepsi, my background was primarily marketing, but I knew I wanted to be a head of a company." Novak knew that there was going to be some reorganization within the company, so he went to his boss and said, "I want to be the Chief Operating Officer at Pepsi Cola Company. Novak's boss reminded him that he knew nothing about operations. "I said, yeah, that's true, I don't. But, if you don't think I'm doing the job in eight weeks, you can fire me, move me back, or do whatever it is, but

I'm committed; I'll do whatever it takes to demonstrate that I'll make up for my lack of knowledge." Novak got the job, and the way he made up for his lack of knowledge was that he went to the people. "I went to the front line. I went out and met with the salespeople, the people in the warehouse, people on the [production] line, and I asked them, what should we do? So, I learned from the people who really knew the business what we should do and then I could use my power, my leverage in the organization, to go back and work on the processes and the tools that would help us to get things done. It was amazing." Armed with this firsthand information, Novak said he could be in a market for one day, sit down at the end of the day, and rattle off four or five things that needed to be worked on. The other thing Novak learned early in his leadership role was the importance of recognition. "People love recognition," Novak says. "This was something I learned in operations when I was the Chief Operating Office of Pepsi Cola. I tell this story all the time; it had a profound impact on my leadership approach and what I think leaders need to do."

Novak explained that he was in a roundtable discussion in a bottling plant in St. Louis about six o'clock one evening. "There were about ten people," Novak recalled, "and I asked these guys to tell me about merchandising. What do we need to do better in merchandising? Who really does it well? And what do they do?" Everyone started talking about one member of the group named Bob, who was sitting directly across from Novak. "They said, 'Well, Bob is the best merchandiser in the whole company.' In about six hours, he showed me more than I learned in six years; he told me how to spin the bottles, and how to go and talk to the store manager to get extra display space." Suddenly, everyone in the room was telling Novak why Bob was the best in merchandising. "I looked over at Bob," said Novak, "and Bob is crying— literally crying. I said, Bob, why are you crying?" And, what was Bob's response? "You know, I've been in this company for 43 years—43 years," he repeated, "and I didn't know anybody felt like this about me." Novak looked around the room and realized there wasn't a dry eye in the place. "I said to myself, you know, if I'm ever a president of a company, if I ever have a chance to be a CEO, I'm going to recognize people like you can't believe." In Chapter 9, we share some of the unique recognition techniques that Novak uses.

"I believe if we stay focused on the people capability of the organization, if we really develop and grow our people better than the competition, we'll satisfy more customers because we'll be smarter at listening to the customer and responding from a marketing perspective. Operationally we'll have our teams more fired up to make it happen at the restaurants, so our sales will go up, our profits will go up, and then when that happens, your stock is going to go up. So, you want to train your people, motivate your people, recognize your people, and give them the tools they need to be successful."

Perhaps it is fitting that the CEO of Deloitte & Touche, one of the world's largest accounting firms, is passionate about putting the value of people into practical terms. Jim Copeland thinks the error in the way some leaders try to view a balance between people and profit issues is that they fail to see the two together. "You see, we see them together," he explains. "People are not a cost. People are an investment, and the idea that good human capital practices are a cost is a fundamental misunderstanding," he emphasizes. "If you've got people that are a cost, you've got the wrong people. Fire them and get other people," he recommends. "If you see people as cost and as a dissolution of profitability, I don't know how you ever reconcile. The better we treat them, the longer they stay. The less cost of turnover we have, the less cost of training and development that we have. The more experienced workforce we have, the more valuable they are in the marketplace for you, and you can charge for their services." Copeland says it's a lot like having a racehorse and deciding that what you really need to do is skimp on food. "The cost of the food, relative to the cost of the horse, is nothing. It's all about whether or not the horse can produce. It's just foolishness!"

Copeland translates the value of people to sound economics. "We believe that we are in a historical time where the cost of products and services, represented by intellectual capital versus physical material, is on a constant up slope; an accelerating up slope," he explains. "Even your most mundane example would be electric blankets." While you may not think electric blankets would have within them much intellectual capital, think again as you hear Copeland explain. "You can buy electric blankets that can keep your feet warmer than they do other parts of your body, and in fact, sense the temperature of different parts of your body and heat the blanket at different levels. All the distinguishing value in the product is based on the intellectual capital," Copeland points out, "because otherwise it's just an electric blanket, and how do you distinguish the value of that product from any other? Well, price. So, you're in a cost war producer environment, unless you can embed intellectual capital in the product in a distinctive way." Copeland adds that it doesn't stop with electric blankets. "Pharmaceuticals are the ultimate example," he states. "Probably 99.9 percent of the value of a specific pill is the intellectual capital in it as opposed to the material in it. A floppy disk is a couple of pennies and the rest is the intellectual property that is embedded in the disk. So, from our standpoint, everything we do needs to be focused on creating an environment where the best and the brightest are attracted, developed, and retained," stresses Copeland. "If we do that, we win."

The Comptroller General of the United States takes a similar position on the importance of people. "In my opinion, any organization has three key enablers to maximize its potential," says David Walker. "In the knowledge-based economy, the most important by far is the people dimension. Especially for the United States, which cannot compete based on wages. In a knowledge-based economy you've got to compete based on productivity and innovation, and the key to that is the people dimension." In the case of the Federal Government, Walker says that for too long the government has viewed people as a cost to cut rather than an asset to be valued. "And, frankly," he points out, "many private sector enterprises until recently have taken the same approach. Now, with slow workforce growth, with the movement to a knowledge-based economy, with an aging society, people are recognizing that they need to change how they've been doing business." Prior to taking on his current role, Walker was in charge of the Human Capital Services Practice for a global accounting firm, so he brings firsthand experience to his government role, and he sees little difference between public, private, or government when it comes to the people issue. "At the GAO for example, 83 percent of our costs represent people costs," Walker explains. "One hundred percent of our assets are people assets. We own this building, but we can't do our job with this building. So, it's just recognizing that people are fundamental and they make the difference between attaining and maintaining a competitive advantage. Even more so in the knowledge-based economy."

To convey his value for people, Walker gave some signals early on that interpersonal relationships would be less formal and more down-to-earth. For one thing, he did lots of walking around to other people's offices rather than summon them to his office. "I'm real, not just a title," he explained. Then he set a new tone at his first executive staff meeting with about 20 top executives. Walker said that when he walked into the conference room, "They were literally sitting at attention; suits buttoned and sitting in the same chairs they'd been sitting in for I don't know how many years. I came in, and before I sat down I took off my coat and hung it on the back of the chair. It was the first time in 50 years anybody had taken their coat off [for an executive meeting]." Walker said he could see the shock in the people's faces. "I said, look, we're not here to impress each other, we're here to get our job done. If you're more comfortable taking off your coats, feel free." Now they actually have business casual. "When we started business casual, there were banners," Walker said. "We hadn't had one business casual day in 70 years. Now we have business casual all the time."

For Walker's second meeting with the executive committee, he entered the room with a plain old coffee mug. "I think it was the first time anyone had seen a Comptroller General drink from anything but china," he laughed. And the third meeting resulted in another, more inclusive change. Five division heads would come to a meeting, one person for each division who represented hundreds of people. They would come to talk about all the different work they had going on from those hundreds of people, Walker explained. "They would have binders this thick," Walker gestured, pointing out several inches. "Then they would come up and make a presentation to about eight executives. This is ridiculous, I said. I can imagine how many hours went into putting the binder together and briefing and briefing. We're going to you from now on; you're not coming up here anymore, we're going to your floor. You bring whoever you want to the meeting and I don't want to see these binders. We need to talk to whoever we need to talk to and get the facts." He opened up the process and went straight to the frontline people. Why be so people-oriented? "It helps me relate to people, and it helps them relate to me," Walker explains. "I'm a people-oriented person. I'm head of an organization, but I'm leading people. When you get right down to it, it makes a lot of sense."

PASSION FOR A GREATER PURPOSE

It wasn't uncommon to hear many of the leaders express that while their organization has a practical need to operate profitably, they also hope and desire that in leading financially stable and productive companies, they can serve a greater purpose.

Dr. Alvin Rohrs demonstrates a total commitment to his passion. "Only lunatics work for nonprofits that are in the toilet," Rohrs says. "Which is what I did when I took over SIFE—Students In Free Enterprise. So you know I had to have a passion for the organization and a belief in it that it could be something bigger and bolder down the road. If I didn't have a passion for what we are doing, it sure wouldn't be worth all the heartache and the struggle to get there," he says.

Rohrs took over the CEO position for the nonprofit educational organization at a time when a recession saw charitable contributions drop and when the head of the organization had to start spending considerable time with his son, who had been diagnosed with leukemia. Saddled with insurmountable difficulties, the organization dropped from donations of $450,000 a year down to $85,000, and its participating schools had dropped from about 100 to 18. Rohrs had been a student in the SIFE program when he attended college. He had gone on to graduate from law school and returned to his undergraduate college to head up a Free Enterprise Institute where, as part of his duties, he would become an advisor for the SIFE team. When fall training began, the SIFE CEO told Rohrs that unless somebody else could take over leadership of the organization, it would be the last year. Discouraged by the news, Rohrs talked to the Chancellor at his college who agreed they couldn't let such a great program die. To help, the college kept Rohrs on the payroll for a couple of years and gave him space and a secretary. Rohrs worked to rebuild the SIFE organization and in 1985, Sam Walton, Wal-Mart's founder, learned about the organization and decided to support it by volunteering the involvement of one of his senior executives, Jack Shewmaker. That was a turning point for SIFE. Today, the organization's program is active in 750 universities throughout the United States and 250 colleges in 20 foreign countries. (For more details about SIFE and how it operates today, read about it in Appendix A.)

Rohrs says that through the years, as he has watched great leaders like Jack Shewmaker and Sam Walton from Wal-Mart and Jack Kahl of Manco, he has learned from them that, "If you are real passionate about what you are doing and about the mission of the company and what the company is all about, or the organization, it really is contagious and it energizes other people. I don't think that people want to follow a leader who doesn't have a passion for what they're doing." To describe his passion about the greater cause that his organization is serving, Rohrs points to the stories he shares with his SIFE staff.

"I think that the thing that inspires our people is when we tell our team about a SIFE team in Mexico that helped this village through the way they helped them run a local business. That they increased the average income in that village from 5 pesos a day to 25 pesos a day, and that they literally increased the GNP of that village by 500 percent a year. The village went from survival peasants to middle class like that—six months and bingo. You explain that to the lady that stuffs the envelopes that got the SIFE team to go. It's like, if you hadn't put that letter in that envelope and put it in the mailbox, they'd have never heard about us. When you're sitting there licking stamps and licking envelopes, you need to know that it's boring and it's mundane, but without you, we don't get this thing done. I want them to know what their role is in the big picture and what they get out of it in terms of whom they really are helping. It's kind of like at the hospital. The doctor gets credit for saving the life, but if it wasn't for the janitor that kept the room sterile, the guy would have died. So make sure the janitor knows that we're glad he kept this room clean." Rohrs points to some very specific greater good that is served by the organization. "Our SIFE teams reach three million school kids each year. They reach close to a million other university students every year. If you want that kid to really understand Economics 101, supply and demand and all that, you put him in charge of teaching that to a third grade class. He's going to walk away knowing that better than anything else. That's really what we do. We want the students to learn leadership, teamwork, and communication, and we say we do that by having students learn, practice, and teach the principles of free enterprise. We take all of this head knowledge they've gotten out of the classroom and we say, now take that marketing class you just had and go out there and help that guy opening up his new café down on the corner. See if you can help him market his café better. Suddenly they find out there's a big difference between a business plan and what really happens. It's really putting legs under everything that they learn in the classroom." To watch that successfully happen not just in the United States, but in Malaysia, Korea, Kazakhstan, Uzbekistan, Brazil, and a host of other countries, gives continual fuel to Rohrs's passion for making a difference and championing a greater cause.

Even for-profit firms demonstrate a passion for serving a greater good when they commit themselves to causes within the community. Len and Debby Gaby have done this from the onset of launching their business in Phoenix, Arizona. In four years, Sleep America grew from 1 retail location to 17 and, despite entering an already heavily penetrated market, has become the largest retailer of mattresses in the Southwest. They even named their store based on their greater belief that what they are selling is less of a product than it is good sleep. "When you feel like you are really helping people, as our passion is to help people, it's a perfect application for us to be in this business, because it has been found that longevity is determined by how well you sleep," said Debbie. The co-owner is so passionate about the importance of sleep that she even teaches sleep seminars for the public. Debbie has become a celebrity from appearing in all of their commercials. That merely augments the community efforts. Part of every television commercial is devoted to help promote local charities and Debbie's visibility helps draw participation when Sleep America sponsors in-store charitable fundraisers. Among the charities supported by Sleep America and the Gabys is Florence Crittenton, a private home for young women. They are helping to raise $7 million for an expansion program for the home. They also donate all the new mattresses to local charities like the Ronald McDonald House and the Sojourner's Center, a center for domestic violence victims. For other organizations, it's involving their store or staff for fundraisers like the Alzheimer's and Arthritis Foundations, or the time they recruited 25 policemen to wear Sleep America hats and uniforms to walk in a walkathon because it was on a Saturday and they couldn't ask any staff to participate because they needed them all to work in the stores. Debbie says she spends 75 percent of her time doing things for the community. How does she decide on the charities to which she devotes her time and resources? "I just follow the heart," she responds. "Sometimes there's no logical reason why I'm doing something, but the heart says we should be there."

The Gabys also feel environmentally responsible, so before they even started their business in Phoenix, they analyzed the market. "We visited St. Vincent de Paul, a local charity, and told them that we wanted to give them our consumers' old mattresses," Debbie explained. They told the organization that when customers would purchase a new mattress, Sleep America would give the old mattress to St. Vincent de Paul and give a tax deductible receipt to the customer for making the donation. So the organization agreed and a process was set up to refurbish and sanitize the mattresses so the organization could distribute them as needed. "It's been a very, very successful program for them and us because we keep our mattresses out of the landfills," said Debbie. Once the stores were open and the program began, a local reporter decided to do a story on the donation program. The Gabys had no idea exactly how many mattresses they might collect over one weekend. So they held the mattresses in a truck over the weekend to see how many were accumulated. Even the Gabys were surprised. When they counted, 400 mattresses were on the truck. It's been very profitable for St. Vincent de Paul, and the Gabys say the organization loves the program.

Whether it's for the business, the people, a greater cause, or all three, true leaders are motivated to lead with a genuine sense of passion.

EXPLORE AND DISCOVER

- Are you passionate about the purpose of your business?

- How do you demonstrate your passion to others?

- As a leader, how do you convey to your people the important role they play in your organization?

- How open are you about displaying your passion?

- How often do you go outside of your own group to solicit ideas and possible solutions?

- What do you do to foster teamwork?

- How often do you spend time talking to frontline employees about their opinions?

- What value do you place on your people?

- What excites you the most about what you do?

- How involved are you in outside community activities?

3

See What Is
Not Yet Visible

True leaders tend to be more strategic than tactical in their thinking. They think in possibilities—what can be that isn't yet visible to others. They have an uncanny ability to sift through volumes of data and selectively ferret out meaningful information to spot trends. They do this with not only their own industry information, but with developments within other industries that may have impact on their own industry's future. One of their greatest strengths is to integrate new knowledge with old to envision better methods, better techniques, and better ideas. They are comfortable with ambiguity and see the possibilities brought forth by the challenge of change. While they have a strong ability to see the big picture, they also possess the systemic thinking to fit all the pieces of the puzzle together to accomplish their desired results. When customers talk about problems and challenges, they have the ability to hear beyond the words to identify new and potential customer needs.

Vision seems to come naturally to them—partially because they are consciously open to new thoughts and ideas. While they often have a keen awareness of their visioning capability, they are never locked in to their thinking. They remain open to hearing others' visions, realizing that ideas combined can expand and enhance their original thinking.

True leaders are visionaries in the truest sense. And, regardless of whether they are leading within the private or public sector, they are visionary in an entrepreneurial sense. Their visionary ability plays an integral role in how these leaders bring clarity to the direction of their business and to accomplishing their business dreams and goals. It also serves as a basis from which to build the company's culture and the core philosophies from which it operates.

BUILDING THE VISION

Terri Bowersock is a classic visionary. By all practical accounts, this woman was not predicted to succeed in the business world. Bowersock's most vivid memories from school are bold red pen marks on her homework with words like *poor work* and *lazy*. When high school SAT scores were posted, everyone could see that she was truly a dummy. School for Terri Bowersock was a very difficult and unpleasant experience. But was she dumb? Not really. She was, however, dyslexic—born with a learning disorder that causes the left side of the brain to recall letters and numbers out of place. Without understanding and proper training, dyslexia impairs the ability to read. Because Bowersock had learned to fake her way through much of the learning process, she was able to get through two years of community college by focusing on discussion groups rather than writing assignments. But when she tried to continue her education at Arizona State University, she lasted only two months. She knew she would have to get a job. Because she couldn't fill out a job application, she became entrepreneurial and sold cold drinks and sandwiches outside the tennis court at a resort in

Phoenix where her mother worked. Later, her mother secured the concession for a gift shop at another resort, and Bowersock managed the shop while her mother taught tennis. That experience taught her that while she might not be able to read or spell, she could sell. And she did have a wonderful, imaginative mind.

One day following a visit to a family friend, who operated a small consignment shop, Bowersock got a big idea. She then created a business plan to convince her mother of the idea. Because she couldn't spell, she drew the plan with crayons and colored pencils, showing pictures of what the store would look like and the national locations it would one day have. With nothing more than a picture in her mind, her hand-drawn business plan, her mother's living room furniture, her own bedroom furniture, and a $2,000 loan from her grandmother, Bowersock started Terri's Consign and Design Furnishings. That was in 1979. Today the business, which includes a franchise company and a real estate and investment company, boasts 17 locations nationwide. "I built it into a $30 million business without taking out one loan from a bank," she states proudly, emphasizing that she knew from the very beginning that her stores were going to be located nationwide—it was part of her vision. "The real key is to know your dream and to visualize it every day. That means that you absolutely believe it," she says. "I knew it in my soul. I didn't know how I was going to get there, but I always knew that there was going to be that day. If a leader does not know where they're going, who's going to follow?" she asks. "Successful people understand that their mind has the power to determine their future. They do not allow their thoughts to control them. Instead, they control their thoughts." Bowersock says people frequently comment that they bet she never thought her business would get so big because she is a woman. "According to today's society and the stereotypes, I should timidly reply that my success was a surprise to me," she says laughingly. "The truth is, however, that from my first crayon business plan, I always knew that my business would get big." In Bowersock's mind, she says, she always envisioned a chain of stores. She pictured people coming in and having a great time finding gently used treasures. "I never let myself doubt my thoughts or imagination. In short, I have simply believed that I can do anything I set my mind to do."

Sleep America's CEO, Len Gaby, is a pretty practical guy. Yet he clearly launched the business with nothing more than a vision. "We had a vision of what it was going to be like before it was even conceived," Gaby explained of the retail company he and his wife Debbie started four years ago in Phoenix, Arizona. As he conveys the story of how the couple began, he paints a vivid picture of a rather bare office in a little warehouse where he used a TV table for his desk. "We had a light hanging from the ceiling and there was a cement floor. I was trying to hire people for a business that didn't exist," Gaby recalls. "I didn't have any fancy presentation boards or anything like that. I just started to talk about what we were going to do and how we were going to do it. We were able to attract marvelous people that are still with us today that were able to conceptualize and see what we were talking about. But, if I didn't have a picture of it in my mind, they never would have gotten an idea of what we were trying to do."

Gaby says the people who grasped his vision tell him that everything he talked about at the inception has come to pass. "Everything we promised, everything we visualized, has materialized. Without exception." Gaby says that he actually wrote a business plan, more for his own benefit and because he felt he had to convince himself that he had really dotted all the Is and crossed the Ts, and to make sure that he was really on target from a financial and business standpoint. He shared the business plan with his CPA, who later told Gaby that in 25 years of experience, Gaby's was the first business plan their firm had ever seen that actually came to pass as it was planned. "Of course, we were dealing in an unknown quantity here because we had no idea what we were getting into," Gaby admits. "That to me says that we saw the future, that we were able to create the future, and that reality is the vision. That's pretty exciting."

VISION TO CREATE AN ENVIRONMENT

When Frank Hennessey became the CEO of MascoTech, a diversified industrial manufacturing company in Grosse Point, Michigan, he found it was not "a cohesive whole." So he pulled together a team of about 25 managers and spent a fair amount of time reinventing the company. "We had to create a vision for our company that everybody would buy into," Hennessey explained. "A leader doesn't need to have the answers, and you have to be very comfortable as a leader knowing that there are people who know more than you and that it's okay not to have all the answers. In fact, that's the way it's supposed to be." What a leader does, according to Hennessey, is to show his vulnerability but stay steadfast in his commitment to envision. "So what we created here was very simple, but very powerful," he said. "We created our vision, which is people creating exceptional value. When you get into defining what that means, you start off by talking about people. People are the most important aspect of any vision.

"We have people who truly make us unique as a company because of their experiences, their intelligence, their competencies, their commitment, their behavior, and their willingness to be a support for each other's success. It's all about people. When you have people who are absolutely energized and empowered, then there isn't anybody that's going to beat you in the marketplace. If you stay focused on what it is the company is committed to, you will be successful.

"The first part, people, is a very powerful part of our vision. Creating is an action verb. It means people doing something—actually creating. That empowers people when they understand that they are expected to create. Then when we talk about value, that's the whole value equation. That's really where the rubber meets the road. The value equation relates to everybody. It's about creating shareholder value—because if you can't make above average return to your shareholders, you will, in the long run, not succeed. And you can't make an exceptional return to your shareholders if you're not satisfying the expectations of your customers, day in and day out. You have to absolutely be dedicated and committed to new and innovative thinking. So the vision—*people creating exceptional value*—just sounds like four words. But, if you live by it, it becomes part of your coaching program and it becomes part of your everyday management style. If you go out and visit the plants and walk the floor and meet with the people, then they all get it. You can't go into any one of our plants and not see people creating exceptional value posted somewhere or not see people living that as our vision. When you look at the way the organization has transformed itself, you can see that it's [the vision] successful—it's powerful—it's true leadership."

VISION FOR CHANGE AND GROWTH

When Radio Shack conducts its annual survey to determine how engaged its people are, one question always ranks off the chart: How much do you trust and respect Len Roberts? "The reason it does," says the Chairman and CEO, "is because people understand where we're going, the strategy, and the vision. They understand why we're doing what we're doing and why we have partnered with different major corporations. They know because it fits our strategy." Roberts says he thinks he's a skilled public speaker and quite good at writing, "but what I think I'm really good at is seeing a strategy."

From the moment Roberts took over the top leadership role at Radio Shack, he realized that the real strength of the organization had nothing to do with products and nothing to do with price. "The real strength was the fact that the American public, while they liked technology, was intimidated by it. If someone had researched it back in 1992, they would have noticed that the American people didn't understand it [technology]. The research shows that what people really like about Radio Shack is not the price, not the fact that we have great products, but a simple thing—they liked the people. They were able to come into our stores and ask a simple question about how to connect a VCR to a TV and what was needed to do it. And our people were knowledgeable." Roberts saw clearly that the company's mission was not to sell products but to sell answers. "The mission then becomes not to be the technology store," Roberts said, which was how the brand was viewed when he arrived at the company. "And it wasn't to demystify technology for the elite or the folks who understood technology. It was to demystify technology for the mass market." That's when the company came up with it's advertising slogan: If you've got questions, we've got answers. Roberts's ability to see what others had not changed the entire direction of the company.

Bruce Simpson, who left a Fortune 500 telecommunications company to lead a fledgling technology company in San Jose, California, believes that from a leadership standpoint, the biggest value he brings to his people is keeping them focused on what the company is all about—what the bigger picture is—and helping them to set meaningful priorities in that context. "It's also the most motivating," Simpson confessed, relating to shifts in the ever changing technology market. "We've gone through a lot of change. A year ago, things were kind of blowing and going and money was flowing freely. Things have changed substantively. And I've got a lot of people that work for me, many of them younger people who have never known of the down cycle. So all the changes cause a lot of uncertainty for people. That's one of the challenges of leadership. It's a lot easier to motivate people when things are going great. The real challenge is to make sure people stay motivated and focused when you're starting to run into some bumps and challenges along the way." To make sure employees had clarity and understanding about the market shifts and their impact on the company, Simpson held two meetings—one on the West coast and one on the East coast. "I can't afford to have people not focused on the right things," he explained. Simpson felt the outcome was incredibly motivating. "Having a big-picture view is so critical as enablers for an overall organization to be successful. Somebody has to be able to provide that to people." In Simpson's view, that's the job of the leader.

"It's easier for a senior leader to have a view of the big picture because you interface with all the things that would give you a big-picture view, whereas somebody farther down in the organization has a more difficult challenge. In terms of where I sit as the CEO, you think of the people that I dialogue with on a regular basis—certainly my investors as represented by the board, industry analysts, customers, and employees. I'm kind of at the heart of all the strategy discussion. So having a big picture is a little easier for me simply because I've got the central position that has input from all of these areas." Add to that Simpson's confession that he's not a very detail-oriented person. "I tend to gravitate toward ideas and concepts as opposed to gravitating toward the details. I have other people that I work with that immediately want to solve the problem and get into the details of what the task is. Those are complementary skill sets. You have to have both."

Simpson says an important issue in the whole process is openness. "I'm always open to new ideas and possibilities, and I don't tend to get locked in one thing, even though I may espouse a strategy and direction. I'm also willing to understand that we live in a very dynamic world and things change quickly. So you have to be open to new input and new ideas. The balance there is not to confuse people that need certainty. I live in a very gray world, and I'm very happy living with a lot of ambiguity. I also have a lot of people on my team today that have a more difficult time looking at that, and they want more certainty—tell me what you want me to do, let me go out and do it." To accommodate the need for certainty, Simpson says he lives in a world of scenarios. "I try to develop multiple views of the future that have some reasonable probability of happening," he explains. Simpson then thinks about, and mentally tests, each scenario for its workability in the business. If they work, great, if they don't, that doesn't mean they won't be pursued. "But, I want to know if one of the other scenarios starts to develop, how do we quickly change to react to that? So I have a contingency plan in the back of my mind." Simpson also admits that the leader's issue is not so much the process of getting the big picture, but communicating it. "I think what is far more important is the communication aspect of it and making sure that the rest of the people that are on the team know what your big picture is."

Sometimes the leader's vision needs to have flexibility. Jim Copeland found this out when two partners at Deloitte & Touche told him they wanted to start a temporary employment firm. "I said, it's off strategy, down market, no thank you, good-bye." But the regional partner didn't give up. He called Copeland back, urging him to look at the business plan. Once again Copeland responded, "It's off market, it's down market, it's off our strategy, why would I want to do this?" The partner was persistent. "I don't think it's as far off strategy as you think, and it's a great business plan. You ought to see it," the partner insisted. So Copeland finally looked at the plan and concluded, "It's off market, it's off strategy, and it's the best business plan I've ever seen and we're going to build it and sell it." The company invested $250,000 into the concept. Nine months later they had their original investment back, the next year they got a $2 million return in cash, and the following year they sold it for $50 million. "We celebrate that," Copeland exclaimed. "We're just about to do a story on the success of these two guys because this is exactly how you create and build culture—you catch somebody doing something good and you celebrate it."

Jack Kahl quotes the Bible, reminding us, "Without vision, the people shall perish." The Manco founder thinks that visioning is the primary task that a leader must do to build and sustain a successful organization. "And, if you have a correct and good vision, the people will believe it and follow it." Kahl says he can't explain how a leader develops vision, but he believes it is an accumulation of life's learnings mixed with a dream. "I can't tell you which part is learning and which part is a passion of believing in your own ideas," Kahl says. "I think a lot of people have ideas and visions, but what most people fail at is they don't have the inner conviction to dare to tell others about it because they're afraid. So, for whatever it is, I think the minute you get through that barrier of self-fear or worrying about what other people think—I think there's a psychology to leadership that says you have to start somewhere. I'll give you a perfect example," he says.

Kahl tells a story about being invited by Sam Walton to attend a Wal-Mart Saturday morning meeting. He had heard about the meetings and had heard about this cheer they all did, and he was very excited to be able to go and see firsthand what he had always heard about. At the meeting, Kahl watched everyone get up and do the cheer—give me a W, give me an A, and so forth. When they came to the hyphen in Wal-Mart, everyone bent their knees and did a little squiggle, like a twist. "Sam got me up and did it with me," Kahl recalled. "But I forgot to do this little squiggle, and they all laughed when I forgot it." Kahl loved the energy that the cheer had created, and he envisioned how that same energy might be translated to his own company. "The cheer was something that felt good there," Kahl said, "Yet I just felt I couldn't bring it back with me." For days the picture of the Wal-Mart team's spirit wouldn't leave Kahl's mind, so one day he changed his mind. "I thought, from now on, I'm going to do the cheer at Manco." So Kahl put a memo out announcing that two new things would be introduced in the company—a Saturday meeting with the executives and middle management from 7:30 AM to 9:30 AM. He also let them know he expected them to be out of the building by 11:00 AM so they could spend the rest of the day with their families. Then he told them that they would do a company cheer. On the Thursday before the meeting, Kahl's secretary came to him. "If you do what you said you're going to do in this memo," she told him, "two-thirds of the people in this company are talking about quitting, and I'm one of them." Kahl listened, then he told her to go back and let all those people know that he hoped they would have a nice career somewhere else because, "We're going to have this meeting on Saturday mornings."

Kahl confessed that he worried if anyone would show up Saturday morning. "That's how hard it is to effect change. That's why you've got to stick with your guns," he said. Well, everybody showed up. "I'll never forget it," Kahl recalled. "We still laugh about it. If you could put daggers in every eyeball, they had daggers in their eyeballs for me. And there I stood, and I said, 'Now we're going to start this meeting with a cheer.' They were the most morose group of humans you've ever assembled on a Saturday. But I started out—give me an M—give me an A—then finally M—A—N—C—O. Well, they did it because I wanted them to, but not because they wanted to. But what happened that morning was that they started meeting other people in the company, and they started communicating and discovering that these people were good people. When I closed the meeting, I closed it with a cheer, and it was much easier to do and it was much louder. And, even though the meeting was over at 9:30 AM, many of them didn't want to go. Some of the people from the very first meeting caught hold of the new kind of feeling that was there. They liked it so much, they didn't want to leave. Every week it became easier. Now, it's impossible to think of any other way to run the company than to start every meeting with a Manco cheer."

Sometimes it's important to inject new vision just to avoid compliancy. Enherent's CEO, Dan Woodward, says that after you've failed enough times you have a built-in barometer on what can or could be and what's reasonable and what's not. "I've certainly had my share of successes and failures and I've learned, as many of us do, from those things that I have failed at. Those are the situations that knock you on the side of the head. And I think that all of us have had the opportunity, if the environment is one that is complaisant, to settle into complacency. We all like to be comfortable. I like to be comfortable, too. But comfortable just doesn't get it. Too comfortable can put you in a situation where your competitors or another country or another economy is hungrier than you are. I don't consider myself very good at being a dreamer, but I will throw a lot of things on the wall to see what will stick. I think over time, I've certainly adapted a more realistic view of what's within the realm of possibility, how to validate that and attach some sanity test to say, that's an expectation that I should have—and then challenge yourself to go achieve it. I think you have to believe. Some of it is just internal optimism."

David Walker always tries to look ahead. "I think part of the job of the leader is to try to ascertain what trends are affecting your organization and trying, through reading, external interactions, talking to clients, and speaking with employees and others, to gather as much intelligence as you can and then analyze that and come back and say, 'What are we trying to accomplish, and how best can we do that to capitalize on our competitive advantages?'" It's a process that works for Walker at the U.S. General Accounting Office.

VISION FOR FOCUS

At BHE Environmental, Inc. in Cincinnati, Chairman and President John Bruck puts his senior management team through a process each year to reinforce the company's vision and to establish desired strategies and goals for the coming year. To begin crafting the company's vision, mission, strategy, and goals, Bruck throws out ideas and filters them through his leadership team. "We would recraft different pieces of it, and then we would put them back together into a concise picture of what the whole organization wants to do," Bruck said. "That resulted in two things. One was, we did a very thorough performance appraisal of everybody in the company to make sure that everybody understood what their performance was, relative to their individual goals and the goals for the whole company. The other thing we did was to develop detailed group plans. Some of those plans overarch others. But all those plans were compiled into a full company business plan, so every single person knows what to do and how to do it so they are in the same basic direction as the company. As part of that, we asked people what they thought the most important things were that they did, and the most important things that the company could do to be able to reach our vision through our mission. From that, we developed a list of priorities. And, depending on where you are in the organization, you may change a strategic priority."

Using the list of about 20 strategic priorities, Bruck conducted an exercise with key managers. He gave the top managers five pieces of BHE currency called Power Dots, and he asked them to spend their Power Dots on the strategic priorities to which they thought Bruck, as the leader, should allocate his time and company resources.

"Based on that, would you think the most important two or three strategic priorities identified should be my charge?" Bruck asked. "Of course," he says, answering his own question. "So, if the team spends their Power Dots to indicate that one priority is more important than the other, that's where I should spend my time. In turn, when I spend my time on that priority and I ask for help in the organization, they will know why, because we, as a company, decided that that's the most important things that we are doing this year." Bruck says this document now becomes a critical tool in his leadership decision making for the year.

Much in the way that John Bruck pulled from his management team to build on the vision from a planning standpoint, Lou Smith, President and CEO of the Ewing Marion Kauffman Foundation, believes it is important to draw from others to create the vision. "Leaders who make a difference, in my opinion, have an ability to pull from their own experiences, and also from others' to create a compelling direction for the organization," says Smith. "Where I think we fall down is if we don't also pull from others, because if I can't get most of our associates to believe in the vision, then it is mine. What I would suggest is that the power of this visionary leader is not that he or she has to have so much [vision], but that she or he has to develop it in concert with enough other people that you are all going down the same path. There is no substitute for passion, energy, the ability to energize, and the ability to create an environment in which others believe—I mean really believe."

Even when things are working well, Gary McDaniel, CEO of Chateau Communities, believes good business is challenging the status quo and looking for fresh, new visions. "It seems to me that you need the ability to be able to say, well, even if it is working, is there a better way? I've particularly noticed as the organization gets bigger, the inertia gets bigger, and everybody tends to be pretty content with being able to just keep doing what they've been doing. The reality is, you can't do that. I'm firmly convinced that if you don't do new things and move forward and take new initiatives, that there's an atrophy that sets in. I think, from an organizational standpoint, atrophy and inertia are what really kill things." To challenge inertia, McDaniel says he brings a lot of crazy ideas to people to think about or he tries to push for some initiatives or alternatives that may or may not work, but at least get people looking in a different direction. "Depending upon how I feel about these things, depends upon how hard I push for them," he admits. "But, you know, I just think that there are always new ways you can do business—bringing in thoughts from conferences or articles, or the way other people look at things differently tends to be helpful too. A lot of times it's the expert from out of town that tends to get the attention, so it's great to bring in that expert in various ways." McDaniel doesn't think this kind of idea probing is necessarily best done in formal meetings. "I'm not sure it's even done with direct reports," he confesses. "I tend to try to do this a lot with a broader range of folks. I find this most effective in one-on-one conversations—traveling with people, airplane time, going to dinner, and when you're on the road, meeting folks at a convention, or driving around in the car looking at properties." McDaniel believes that a big part of his job is to make sure that people are challenged to do better. "Part of that challenge is that you have to give them a little bit of a road map—here's where I think we can go, and here's where I think we can do better. Then allow them to figure out ways to do it."

Irv Hockaday sums up the importance of vision by saying, "You have to not only explain to people where you are going, but they have to understand why that is the particular place you want to get to, and hopefully the justification is persuasive or compelling. In the best of circumstances, it is uplifting." Without clarity, the vision can be abstract for some people. The Hallmark CEO says he has used the analogy at times that, "leaders need basically three things. They need binoculars to see into the distance; they need a megaphone, because once you get started, you need to be a cheerleader and a supporter; and, while hopefully you won't have to use it too often, a riding crop to pick up the pace when people aren't out of the starting gates. As you know," Hockaday says with a laugh, "today you just have to move faster."

EXPLORE AND DISCOVER

- How clear to you is the vision for your business division or unit?
- How often do you have an opportunity to talk about it with others?
- How do you use the knowledge of that vision when making decisions?
- Knowing the vision, how does it help you to spot industry trends?
- What do you do to spot trends and broaden your awareness?
- What future scenarios can you develop for your area of the business?
- How can you bring others into that scenario-developing process?
- What changes are happening in your industry, and how do they relate to the vision?

- A year from now, what would you like people to say about your contribution to the vision?

- What are other industries or your competitors doing that could be adapted to bring fresh thinking to your organization's vision?

4

Care Enough to Connect and Convey

True leaders must be powerful communicators to connect with their people and convey what's important. They don't necessarily have to be charismatic, but they must be compelling in their ability to help others capture their passion for the company's vision and purpose and to embrace the cultural values thatdrive the company's success. All too often, an integral part of the communication process is ignored—listening.

Listening is critical to a true leader's success. Lou Smith thinks listening is so critical that he says you must listen to learn and then to lead, and it must be done in that order to be truly effective. "There are a lot of people who have great talent both as individuals and leaders, but we don't know it all," says the President and CEO of the Ewing Marion Kauffman Foundation. "The first thing we need to do is understand the environment, not by talking, but by listening, by learning, and then you lead. I'm just a firm believer that if you try to reverse that process, it's almost always

fatal for the individual or the organization, or both." Smith believes this is true whether you have been in the organization a
long time or if you are new to a leadership role. He says that ego-
balanced leaders are those who are willing to accept that not only
do they not know everything, but they are not expected to know
everything. "So," he says, "if they listen and they learn, then they
combine what they know with what others know, and they are
able to energize and excite the organization." Smith also points
out that it is important to listen to the right people. "The right people aren't just those who have particular titles or positions," he
clarifies. "The right people are those who have the relevant information. A prime example for me was early in my career at Allied Signal as a junior engineer. It wasn't just engineers I needed
to listen to; I needed to listen to the technologists, because the
technologists had to take what was in somebody's mind and put
that into production. They had to take your ideas and dreams and
make them a reality. The same thing is true here," he notes, referring to the foundation.

One of the ways Smith implements this broad-based listening
concept is by having Chats with Lou. Five times a year, he con-
venes a group of 30 to 50 associates to spend time listening to their
ideas, their suggestions, and just about anything they want to talk
about. To ensure that the environment is one of total listening, the
organization has built a room modeled after an Indian kiva. The
seating is tiered in a circular design so that everyone can see Smith
when he sits on a stool in the middle and so that he can easily see
each of the participants. Smith is quick to point out that there are
no audiovisual gadgets in the room—no microphones, no speakers, no projectors, no screens—nothing to distract from the important ability to fully listen. "Create an environment wherein
you can hear what is being said, and therefore you can be in a position to provide some vision, some leadership, some direction,
some substance to what you've heard," Smith recommends.

Using the Chat with Lou format, Smith gives every associate
a chance to talk with him, which provides a chance for Smith to

listen for important information from which to learn—then lead. Smith also schedules one-on-one time with his core leadership team every other week. "We see one another numerous times a day," Smith says, "but this is specific time set aside on the calendar to talk about issues, opportunities, and problems." To ensure that listening really happens, Smith points out that you must always close the communication loop. "Closing the loop does not mean that I have acted on what you have said," he explained. "It does say that I have taken it into account. For our associates, it's those regular feedback sessions. I think what people do is they sum up all that has been talked about and then they say, 'Have I or have I not been heard?' We provide a balanced decision-making process that suggests that the decision maker is responsible for getting all relevant input information before he or she makes a decision. Now, sometimes that relevant input is only from some board members, and sometimes it is from the associates. But you, as the decision maker, are never removed from making the final decision."

We found that listening breaks into three basic areas: listening to learn, to encourage, and to grow.

LISTENING TO LEARN

Listening is absolutely essential to Gary Nelon, Chairman and CEO of First Texas Bancorp, Inc. "I don't think that anybody can gain either a sense of purpose or direction from the external world or have a feel for whether or not your message is being heard or felt across the whole organization without getting real feedback from those people," says Nelon. "If you leave the listening part of the equation out of the picture, you have lost a very important aspect of what it takes to be leading." How does Nelon ensure that listening is demonstrated? First, he says, you have to make yourself available. "You have to actually practice the art of listening," he said. "You have to not only give time to the people that you need feedback from, but show that you genuinely care

about what they have to say. You don't have to have all the answers preprogrammed in your head." Nelon says that most communication conflicts that he has seen in business happened when someone had not taken the time to understand fully the other person's side, and they were unwilling to spend the energy to come to a common ground by restating what they thought they heard or asking some important questions. "Let me understand what you're saying. Or, is there something more that needs to be on the table other than what's been said?" are typical probing statements or questions he suggests. Once this back and forth clarification happens, Nelon says, people really get invested. If you have listened to people and let them know that you have really heard them, "They wind up feeling like they have created the solution through the feedback you gave them, and all of a sudden the harmony you have been working toward, a mutual goal in a complicated business environment, gets a lot better."

Chairman and CEO Len Roberts says his heroes are the ordinary people at Radio Shack who are doing extraordinary things. "I've learned the most from them," he says. "I've been inspired by them, because I have learned the business through their eyes and I've learned the issues through their eyes. My heroes are every single store manager in this company who comes face to face with a customer in handling the issues." Frank Hennessey says the process of learning consists of generous listening, straight talk, and mutuality of commitment. "The power of inquiry is enormous. When you learn that the power of listening is as great as the power of speaking, you begin to make a difference in people's lives," says the CEO of MascoTech. American Italian Pasta Company CEO, Tim Webster, says it is also important that when you listen to your people, you really listen to them. "Keep your humility about you. Ask them, then let them finish," he says. "Don't start to tell them why they are wrong before they get a chance to explain what they are feeling."

John Bruck admits that he probably doesn't listen as much as he should. "If you were critical of me, I think that's one of the

things I could definitely improve on. But I do listen a lot." To demonstrate his commitment to listening to learn, Bruck says, "As a leader, if I'm going to be successful, I cannot have the attitude that I'm the smartest guy in the world—in fact, to the contrary. I think I have to surround myself with people who are a lot smarter than me." Managing smart people, Bruck admits, is a real challenge—one that he believes works best when you show them professional, technical, and intellectual respect. That involves listening. "If you have a world-class archeologist who gets an award for work he did, as a leader, you'd better go read that work and you'd better be able to go sit down in his office and talk with him about it and ask some questions and listen to the answers." Bruck sites this as an example because the man who heads up the company's Cultural Resources Group was recognized two years in a row by the Secretary of the Interior for his expertise. He is one of the few archeologists who can do what is called deep testing. He has the ability to dig deeper holes and recover culturally significant objects from deeper formations than anybody else in the country. "And you have to know that," Bruck points out. "You have to really understand the report, really understand the issues, really understand what the accomplishment is, and you have to put that in the context of your company." To learn the true significance of all of that requires deep listening.

True leaders are secure enough to admit that they have more to learn and that one of the best ways to keep learning is by listening to their own people.

LISTENING TO ENCOURAGE

Ann Hambly believes listening encourages collaboration, so she listens for diversity of thinking. "I like to hear lots of views," she said. "I like to have all my managers be able to expect a differing view from each other. Somehow I can then take that and get the group to come up with some general agreement. There could be one or two who certainly don't follow the middle, but I try to get the majority of the group to the center. If I can't, I will put the subject aside and come back to it in another setting and try again. I really hear people out," she says. Brent Hardman, who has worked for Hambly for 15 years, following her to different companies through the years, and now to Prudential Asset Resources, confirms Hambly's effective communication skills. "It's really an art the way she treats people," Hardman says. "There are no hidden agendas. She never talks down to you. She'd never raise her voice or lose her cool. I have seen where she will call a group of people together and I know she already knows what the answer is going to be. But she wants them to feel a part of the process, so she'll throw it out and say, here is the problem, help me solve it. They throw out solutions, write things on the board, pros and cons, and pretty soon everyone says, well we think this is the answer. During that process, if someone comes up with a really good reason why it shouldn't go in one direction, she is open to that. She always wants people to be a part of the decision-making process. She always asks for feedback. She never just says, this is the way it is, like so many people do."

Hambly says in the past she worked for people who insisted that they were right and didn't want to hear any input. Often, she said, that resulted in a negative consequence. "If you don't take time to hear people out and listen, you're going to make bad decisions," she said. "Listening, to me, makes me feel there is an openness that I can go back and tell people things that maybe a boss who didn't listen would not. I give every single person equal access to me if they want to come in and meet with me. I give them the same respect I would my boss. My motto has been to treat everyone—every single person—with the same level of respect you would expect. There should be no distinction if they are the receptionist, the secretary, or the file clerk. They are still people doing a job that is important to your success, and if you think they're not, try moving them out for a week." Hambly summarizes up listening like this: "If you know your business and you are a good listener, and you aren't afraid to make decisions and treat people like you want to be treated, I think that is the core makings of a leader. You get good by doing it more and more and more. If you always use these skills, and you listen more, and you are willing to change more, you get better as you go on."

Mike McCarthy also believes in listening to people at all levels and then recognizing them to let them know they've been heard. The Chairman of McCarthy Building Companies, Inc., cites as an example a situation where the company was trying to get a computer problem resolved. A new program would provide immediate access to everyone throughout the company, but it had glitches that weren't getting resolved. One day, he got a call from his Seattle office and found the problem had been resolved. The call came from the Information Technology Department, so McCarthy called to find out who had resolved the problem. He found out the problem had not been solved by the IT department, but rather had been solved by a secretary in the Operations Department. "I called the division president and asked him to tell me about this young woman." On McCarthy's next trip to the West coast, he went to a jewelry store in San Francisco and bought the woman a David Yrman bracelet with a diamond in it. "The next time we had one of our parties in Seattle to celebrate, I called her up in front of the room and told her, 'I just want to thank you for continually doing things for this company that are outside of your job that are very special. We appreciate your intelligence, we appreciate your attitude as far as helping people, and we wanted to give you this little gift.' She was undone!" McCarthy said, "It is very important to listen to what people are doing and to look for the real superheroes who are working in the trenches and who really make things happen."

True leaders look for opportunities to engage in conversations in which they can effectively listen, and by giving the gift of feedback to demonstrate that they did listen, their employees feel encouraged, inspired, and empowered.

LISTENING TO GROW

Listening also plays an important part in consensus building. At its best, consensus decisions can often lead to better outcomes. Jim Copeland learned the power of listening to build consensus when he was with Deloitte & Touche's Atlanta office and became involved in the community as a volunteer. Copeland observed, "It struck me that the methods the volunteers used, like consensus building, and all the ways of bringing a group to a decision, would be even more valuable in an environment where you had the power and authority but didn't use it." He said that he has never really believed that power and authority were particularly valuable tools. He believes that most people worth leading would probably leave the organization if they felt they simply had to follow everything a leader said without having any input. "So I formulated a lot of my concepts about leadership in watching people work in environments where they didn't have the ultimate organizational power and authority, yet they still got an awful lot done." Copeland said the combination of learning by listening to others, without using the power everyone knew you had, became a very powerful combination. "To go around the room and ask, 'What do you think?' You could make the decision yourself, yet you involved others in the process." That's a powerful benefit of listening—one that often yields more fruitful results than when ideas are thrust upon others by the leader.

Jim Nicholson says he learns something every day from somebody by listening. "I think there may be a notion that leaders have all the answers. But, I think the reality is that leaders are really just collectors and synthesizers of information. If you aren't listening, you aren't gathering information. You're working off your own historic prejudices. So it is very important to ask those open-ended questions and get your people to open up and tell you what's really going on. Leaders are good listeners when they're listening at a lot of levels in the organization." The PVS Chemical's CEO believes that every company has a myriad of technical ways to communicate and get feedback, yet there is nothing like being with people at a coffee break or showing up with a couple of dozen of donuts and sitting around to hear what's happening. "You're really there just to small talk, but after a while, people's issues start to percolate once they're a little more relaxed." That is when genuine listening really sets in.

Frank Hennessey learned about a potential safety hazard by listening. It happened shortly after he took over as the new CEO of MascoTech. "We were having trouble at one of our plants, and there was a threat of unionization," he explained. "This plant worked three shifts a day, so I went there at four in the morning and caught the first shift. I spent an hour and a half in conversation with the entire workforce so that they could tell me what wasn't working. I stayed all day long—did the second shift and did the third shift." Hennessey found the experience fascinating. For one thing, Hennessey's guess was that this was a plant at which they had never seen a CEO of the company before—let alone talk to him and have him listen. Second, the workers had never seen anybody stay for 24 hours to meet with all of the people, to walk the floor and talk with people about what they did, and to find out what suggestions they might have for improvements. In one of those sessions, Hennessey learned something very important. When he asked for questions, one of the men handed him a mask and a spray paint bomb. He asked Hennessey, "Could you spray paint with this mask?" Hennessey responded, "There must be a reason that you're asking me this question. What is it?" The man pointed to the label on the paint and said, "If you read the label on that can, you will find that the mask that we have is not effective against this kind of paint for the vapor and the hazardous exposure, yet we're asked to do that." It was an important learning experience for Hennessey. "We were able to honestly dialogue about what was important to this particular person at this time and we were able to reach a conclusion and create a Health and Safety Committee comprised of workers and management to identify all the potential health hazards that might exist in the workplace and to do something about them. That one incident ended up being a major corporatewide health and safety campaign. Even the company's President's Awards were changed so that there is a specific standard of performance around safety that is paramount in every facility. These are the kinds of things that evidence your true concern and caring about people," Hennessey said.

Sometimes listening merely confirms that you're doing things right. Sleep America's CEO Len Gaby shared an experience he had in one of the stores, when he listened while a customer interacted with a sales associate. The customer had just made a purchase and began to tell the sales associate about an experience with one of Gaby's competitors. "After the transaction was over, I went over to this woman and told her I had heard that she had gone to this competitor and decided not to buy there. Would you mind telling me why you didn't buy there?" Gaby asked. The woman told him that while shopping at the competitor she tried something rather unusual and asked the salesperson how he liked working in the store. "It must have been a catharsis for him," she told Gaby, "because he just started to tell me how terrible the people were, how they abused the salespeople, how they even made the salespeople in the store buy their own toilet paper, and went on and on." The woman told Gaby that after hearing all that, she decided not to buy from the company. "That's really fascinating," Gaby told the woman. "I'm sure you asked our associate the same question." No, she hadn't. She said she didn't have to. "He took me up and showed me the letters of appreciation from the community, told me that the owners of the company were nice and it was a great place to work. I never had to ask him, I knew." Gaby said the experience was an incredible lesson for him. It demonstrated the important top down, inside out attitude that goes through an organization and permeates to the public. "When the genuine caring is there, the public knows," Gaby said. "You absolutely can't fake it. It has to be real and it has to be sincere, and you have to live it every day." Listening confirmed this for him.

Listening also translates to repeat customers. Jack Lowe, CEO of TD Industries, says, "We wear our customers out asking them how we're doing. We ask all the time about how we are doing, but then periodically we ask them, what's important to you? How are we doing? How's our best competitor doing? How's the best supplier you do business with doing?' Then you sort of get a matrix on what's important." By listening to their customers, the company has raised the bar. "We won the Texas Quality Award in 1998," said Lowe, "and we're applying for the [Malcolm] Baldridge Award this year."

Bill Matthews of Plante & Moran, LLP, believes that listening is critical to client retention and growth. The CPA firm did a survey of clients when they did their last strategic planning. "We learned some things. We needed to be more entrenched with our clients, more involved with them. More and more, we're doing client surveys," he said. "I don't think most firms listen to their clients as well as they should. I think maybe there's a certain amount of arrogance." Matthews says it's important to listen to customers and encourage them to report what isn't working. The time to ask is not after the client is lost, he points out. The time is all along the relationship. How the client feels is extremely important and the only way to be sure is to probe and listen to what the client really has to say. If you only ask internally, after the client is lost, it's amazing how often a partner will almost always respond that the client was unhappy with fees or that the client was a jerk. "I'm always amazed how many clients become jerks after they've fired us," Matthews says with a laugh. Communicating along the way, particularly listening, helps to avoid these kind of negative situations.

Listening gives leaders a leading edge that fosters new ideas, empowerment, and even an ability to get a jump on the competition.

AFTER LISTENING, COMMUNICATE TO LEAD

To be effective, leaders must clearly communicate. They must communicate to convey the company's vision and its value-driven environment, to encourage and inspire their people, and to keep people continually informed.

"I think enduring organizations are inclusive," says Lou Smith. "Not for any reason other than that's how you become a preeminent organization. Why wouldn't I want to capture the input and the intelligence and the energy of all of our associates rather than just five people who report directly to me with the privilege of having a senior title? Why wouldn't I want to capture input from the newest associate?" Smith explains that he has breakfast with all new associates to establish early on that the foundation operates in an environment in which anyone who comes to his office understands that they work within an environment that is not about hierarchy access, but about everyone bringing ideas to the forefront that are important to the organization. So Smith creates an environment that includes three elements that he terms as *the given* for a successful organization: mutual respect, trust, and integrity. "If you've got those three, you can disagree, but you still respect one another. You know that no matter what the issues are, it's not about personal agendas because our integrity is so high. We are not going to violate any of those. We will make mistakes—we're not perfect—but you can't violate those three." Smith says that what he has come to believe is, "If you are really going to be the leader of the organization, you have got to let the organization get to the same point you are. Even though it may take a little longer in the process, it's theirs." To achieve that takes open, honest, effective communications—including listening.

COMMUNICATE TO CONVEY VISION, VALUES, AND ENVIRONMENT

"It's important to carry the values forward and to say, here's what McCarthy really is about," says Mike McCarthy about his building company. "It's important to be in the field appreciating what people are doing—to see what they've done with their hands and to show some empathy for their problems. It's important to be proud of them for what they've accomplished." To do this, McCarthy says meeting one-to-one helps to establish strong ties to the people on the job site who are solving problems. "Because we have so many projects that may be 500 miles from the nearest regional office, you've got to be there and show that they're a part of the team and they are part of the family, and that you really appreciate what they are doing." McCarthy says that's why in his business they do a lot of "travel to touch." To the extent that the people feel part of the family, he says, they will be more likely to stay with the company. "To the extent that they understand our goals and meld them with their goals, we are more likely to be successful and more productive."

BHE's John Bruck says he sees his leadership role as one of an evangelist. "It's the weekly scripture reading," he says. "It's the constant reminder to folks to align what they are doing with what their goals are, which is attached to the vision and mission and the basic company purpose." Bruck spends a vast majority of his time walking the floor. He rarely has meetings in his office. Instead, he visits with people in their own work areas. "I walk around constantly," he says. "And I walk around our client's operations with our key managers so that they can watch how I behave in front of a client. I take very seriously a hands-on approach to teaching and directing folks in our organization what I can personally contribute to their success."

Irv Hockaday explains that in a world where change is ever present, effective communication is increasingly important. "In good organizations, you can't con people that you know where you're trying to go collectively. There has to be a good reason for it. I think subliminally people are beginning to think that companies change because it is the *flavor du jour*," Hockaday warns. "You have to not only explain to people where you are going, but they have to understand why that is the particular place you want to get to, and hopefully the justification is persuasive or compelling.

In the best circumstances, it is uplifting. So you need to talk to people and engage them on that subject." Sometimes when you do this, Hockaday says, you learn things that you have overlooked or haven't given sufficient weight. "Once you have collaboration on where to go and why it is important to get there, then it becomes very important to explain it within the context of what people in a specific division or department can actually do to help you get the desired outcome." Hockaday says he doesn't know how anything can get done if it isn't communicated clearly. "Then people don't know what the game plan is. I don't think you have to be a charismatic superstar, but you do need to be clear. You do need the courage of your own convictions. To me, if you don't do that well, I don't know how you get anything done at the higher levels."

Hockaday admits that communicating a consistent message clearly isn't always easy within large organizations. One of the things he does to help the flow of information is to have CEO Forums. "We put a notice in the *Noon News,* which is our daily newspaper, that there will be a CEO Forum at a specific time and place, and that everybody is invited to come," Hockaday explains. Often the meeting will address a specific topic. Sometimes it will be a Q & A. Because Hallmark has various locations, Hockaday also goes to where the people are in various parts of the country and has similar meetings. Hockaday concedes that Hallmark has traditionally been a very polite, button-down place, "For literally years," he said, "people wouldn't really ask what would be considered impolite questions, which is usually what they want to know about. They just thought that it was inappropriate. I tried emphasizing that if they didn't ask these kinds of questions, then I couldn't answer them. But that didn't work. Then I started asking those questions rhetorically.

At an early forum, Hockaday set the tone for asking anything by mentioning an incident that that was quite unexpected and a bit extreme. " Right after I got here, there was a rumor that I'd run off with the receptionist," he said with a chuckle. "I was actually on vacation with my wife. That was really extreme. Well, that was actually a blessing in disguise because I could now say, 'Look, I know there are questions you want to ask me and won't, and I want you to ask them. For example, you want to know why I ran off with the receptionist." That really broke the ice. Since then, there has been less reluctance for people to ask about what is really on their minds. Besides breaking the ice that day, Hockaday showed his human side and established an environment of trust. "You can be an ace communicator, but if they don't trust you, you're blowing air," he points out.

Bruce Simpson believes that communicating the big picture to all of the people is a major aspect of leadership. "For me, it's communicating in multiple and different ways frequently," Simpson says. "It's a process issue." Simpson observes that as a company grows and people spend less time with the informal communication processes, conveying information in different formats becomes more important "People learn in different ways," he says. "I tend to be pretty visual. I like charts and graphs. Others like text. Other people like oral. Those are all good ways to communicate, and you have to use them all." What's important, he says, is that communications must be regular, because things change as time goes on. Simpson likes voice mail because he thinks it is a very personal way to communicate. Some people like e-mail because they are more e-mailcentric. "But there is no substitute for face-to-face time. So I like meetings, both in big groups and small groups, because those can be interactive and real-time. The difficult part with other tools, like e-mail or voice mail, is that I don't have a way to assess very quickly if I am communicating accurately. I've had too many examples where I'll write something down and I know exactly what I mean, and an individual reads it and takes a different intent. If I'm sitting here and talking to that same individual, and I say something that he takes in the wrong way, I can tell from his reaction. Or he can ask a clarifying question." Simpson relates a personal example:

Simpson received an e-mail from his COO after a meeting he had held in Memphis where there had been a social get together. At the get together, Simpson had walked up to a table and asked people how they thought the meeting went—did they get good value out of it? "A young lady asked me, 'Well, how do you think it went?' and I said, well, frankly, it didn't meet my expectations. I wasn't pleased with my performance." About that time, the conversation between Simpson and the woman got interrupted. Simpson returned to the woman later and continued. "I tend to be pretty self-critical and set pretty high standards for myself, and while I think the overall meeting went very well and achieved its objectives, with the benefit of hindsight, there are a number of things I would have done differently." Someone overheard the first part of Simpson's conversation, but not the last, and told the COO the next day that Simpson thought the meeting was a failure. The COO passed on to Simpson the comments and Simpson had to explain what really happened. "The same thing happens in e-mail," Simpson says. "It's so easy to take somebody's words out of context and walk away with the wrong message. So, while I think e-mail and voice mail are good communication tools, I always believe there is no substitute for face-to-face interaction."

Tim Webster is constantly reminding his people of American Italian Pasta Company's purpose to be the best for its customers in terms of quality, cost, and service. "We have monthly communication meetings in all the locations where those three elements are the beginning, the middle, and the end. We start the meeting asking someone to restate the purpose of the company, we finish the meeting asking someone to restate the purpose of the company, and we have an open dialogue about how we did during the intervening period living up to those three things. So it is through communication, leading by example, and constant reinforcement of how our actions are consistent with our purpose."

True leaders make sure to put in place a communication process that ensures that the company's vision and purpose are the cornerstones of all actions, and they use a variety of communication tools to convey a consistent message.

COMMUNICATE TO CONVEY RECOGNITION AND TO INSPIRE

At Deloitte & Touche, communicating to one another in a manner that demonstrates respect and teamwork is everyone's responsibility. Jim Copeland says a leader's responsibility is to create an environment where people trust you, believe you care about them, and believe that you are committed to excellence. "We push this down," he said. "We say, if you have a desire to work for a trustworthy organization, you have no right to expect that, unless the people who work directly with you find you trustworthy. So, if you're a senior accountant, don't come to me as the partner on your job and complain because the manager doesn't treat you in an open and collegial way, unless you are certain that the people you are responsible for are treated in an open and collegial way. You have no right to expect that unless you have created that environment around you. We say this cannot be done from the top down. The leadership model has to be there, but that's insufficient. It has to be a matter of having everyone in the organization accept responsibility for creating their work environment, and the truth of that is self-evident."

Copeland believes that cultures are powerful. "In key times, they are a strong competitive advantage. Our culture is a culture that reinforces nimbleness and the ability to make decisions and the empowerment of individual professionals, so it works very, very well." It's not about rhetoric, Copeland says. "It's about what you can demonstrate, prove, and show. We have lower turnover statistics than any of our competitors, and we know that. Those are things you can't fake and you can't deceive yourself about. Our vision is to be the best professional services firm in the world.

Our mission, in the terms of how we are going to get there, is by helping our people and our clients to excel. From that, there are two things that cascade. One is a series of plans beginning with a strategic plan, rolling down into operating plans, and until we get down to the individual role. Then we have a culture that reinforces what we want to accomplish, and you consciously work at creating that culture. The culture informs you where the boundaries of behavior are, and you don't have a bunch of rules because you walk into any office in our firm and you yell at a secretary, and 14 heads will snap around. Nobody has to say anything to you. You know you have just made a mistake. It is a self-reinforcing mechanism. It is a way to avoid having rules, but it still defines the parameters of behavior."

Vicki Henry, CEO of Feedback Plus, Inc., believes there is incredible power in a leader's language. "When someone squelches enthusiasm, it's like pouring cold water on somebody. I think the damage can be very significant. Depending on where they are in their career, I think it can be very lasting damage. The words we say to people are extremely powerful. People remember their bad news. You can give someone ten compliments and one criticism. It's human to pick out the one criticism. I think it can be very damaging to people to in any way let them think that you don't value their opinion, or certainly their creativity. When someone comes up with a new idea, you should really be open to that and handle it very delicately. I say nothing is more contagious than positive people, except negative people."

David Novak believes that honest feedback is one of the greatest gifts a leader can provide. "I think a leader knows that their responsibility to the organization is to develop other leaders. The only way you grow any business is through people. So what a great leader does is have the courage to assess somebody's strengths and weaknesses, and just like in marketing, you take advantage of the strengths and try to make them a core equity for that person. Then you shore up the weaknesses and make sure they don't become fatal flaws. You do that through continual feedback and taking the time to give people the gift of feedback. I think feedback is a tremendous gift and that if you are fortunate enough to work with a true leader, you get it all the time." The Tricon Global Restaurants CEO also thinks feedback is the only way to really build a team. "You celebrate somebody else's idea more than your own," he said. "You get *I* out of your vocabulary, and you put *we* into it. I call it the power of we versus the power of me." Novak says that any leader who thinks that he or she can do everything alone or is smarter than anybody else, is making the biggest mistake a leader can make. "When people feel that a leader thinks they are smarter than everybody else, I think you cut about 75 percent of the intellectual horsepower out of an organization. It becomes very important that you recognize that the best ideas anybody can come up with are their own, and that you realize that your best job is to plant the seeds to bring ideas forward and to recognize ideas of other people versus your own."

To make his point, Novak shares a story told to him by Magic Johnson. Johnson told Novak that when he was a little kid he played basketball, and his team would win a game by about 80 to 20 with Johnson scoring 65 of the points. When the game was over, everybody was mad at him. Then, Johnson told Novak, he learned how to pass the ball, and all of a sudden when they won 80 to 20 and he had only scored 20 points, and everybody else scored points too, everybody was happier at the end. So Johnson decided he was going to be the best passer in the world and make the team great, rather than personally be the number one guy. Novak says that at any point in time a leader is at his or her best when listening to others to build the team. He says he has seen some of the smartest guys in the world, whom he used to be in awe of, flame out because either their people didn't feel the leader was smart, or their people didn't trust the leader so they didn't get involved. "When that happens, your people will destroy you," Novak says. "It's just a matter of time."

Jack Kahl uses quotes to encourage and inspire. "Walt Disney always said the mixture of the old and the new is how you get the new all over again," says Kahl. So when he built a new home for Manco, he had street signs put up for different hallways. "We had Information Highway for one, Renovation Lane was another—that's the marketing department. We had prizes for the best name and we created old-fashioned gaslight type street signs. An old American gaslight look with a new name on it brought into a brand new building provided the best of the old values and gave us sort of a rooted home, so you felt at home the first day you were there. People loved it, and everybody was involved in naming the streets." The other thing Kahl did was to post quote signs throughout the company to help motivate and inspire people. "The first quote I put up was for me," he said. "It was a game I played with myself and still do. I put it over the water cooler so that as you bent down to get a drink of water, you saw it. It said, 'Successful people invest in themselves.' So, think about it—every one of us has to drink water every day to survive, but how many people don't do anything other than the necessary. So my feeling was that every time I went to the water cooler, I would ask myself, 'What am I doing today to improve myself'? Pretty soon I had everybody playing that game for self-improvement. Now, I think there are 223 signs throughout the company." Kahl says when people visit the company, they tell him they love the signs and want copies. He tells them to take what they like, but encourages them to go find their own because they will be more meaningful. "In a house, what do people put in the family room?" Kahl asks. "Pictures of the family," he responds. "Well, our house at Manco is a family, too. So, around here, we have all these things that we want to be reminded of." It is Kahl's way of lifting spirits and encouraging people to grow.

To encourage fairness and equity at Weight Watchers, President and CEO Linda Huett says it's important to get rid of politics. "I think getting rid of politics in an organization is one of the most important things you can do," she says. "Getting rid of the internal politics, the jockeying for position, the trying to score points against your peers so that you can appear to be better. All of that you just have to get rid of very, very quickly." Huett believes that, as a leader, if you see politics and you recognize it, you have to talk openly to the people being political and let them know that it is unproductive. "Usually they're only doing it because they think it's actually going to work," she points out. "And what I mean by work is that they think they will be seen in a better light and that they will have a better chance of promotion. I think you have to show a team that [such behavior] is counterproductive to their advancing." Approaching politics head on communicates a clear message that leadership does not favor a political approach and that teamwork is expected instead.

Len Roberts thinks that today, more than any time before, a leader has to have very good communication skills and be able to put thoughts together very quickly to relate to people. "It's a world that moves fast, and people have to understand quickly. New companies move fast, and you really have to have some great communication skills, and you have to be passionate, and you have to care." Every quarter, the Radio Shack CEO spends three days with about 65 officers just listening, listening, and listening. He also allocates money to train his people. "We put money into our people—in training, in development, in retention—and training, and training, and training. The more courses they take, they get certified. If they get certified, they make more money. Everything is incentivised so they learn, learn, and learn more. Everyone should be investing in their people. Everyone should be training their people. You have to be nuts not to do it." By investing in the development of people, Roberts communicates loud and clear that people are valued and play an important role in Radio Shack's overall success.

Many communication vehicles are available to encourage and inspire people. True leaders use a variety of methods, but all with the same purpose in mind—to demonstrate value and to inspire continued growth.

COMMUNICATE TO KEEP INFORMED

The larger the company, the more challenging it is to ensure that communication flows through the entire organization. "Communication is something we are always fighting, so we work very hard at keeping people informed as to how we are doing and how it affects them and what they can expect," says Bill Matthews. "I don't want to tell them at the firm conference next June that we didn't have a very good year. They need to know right now how we're doing. We keep them informed because they have a stake in this, too. So we spend a lot of time and effort communicating how the firm is doing, how they are doing, and what it means for them." At Plante & Moran, Matthews also makes a habit of visiting every office. "Usually when I visit an office, we have a staff get-together—breakfast or lunch or something—and we talk about how the firm is doing and they ask questions. The big thrust is really making everyone feel like an integral part of the team."

Jack Lowe says, "We've got newsletters, we've got open-book management, we've got no doors, and we've got meetings out the kazoo. We have three newsletters, one weekly and two, three times a year. We have lots of departmental meetings, typically monthly, some quarterly that are a couple of hours at a pop." Lowe also schedules time with groups of a couple of dozen people at a time for three-hour meetings. "So about every other week, I spend from seven to ten o'clock in the morning with a group of employees," Lowe says. "Typically, we do a lot of eating together. I believe in breaking bread as relationship building. So often it involves a meal—either breakfast or lunch. We have a little card that has four things on it—what are your aspirations? There are a couple of questions around that. And, what does the company do that is keeping you from reaching your aspirations? It's just a conversation about how it's going. This is done annually—typically in the first quarter." Using the card provides an easy way to get the conversation started and helps to focus the time spent. (See Appendix C for the full copy on this card.)

At The Container Store, VP meetings help to keep departments up to date. "We cover everything that is going on in the business," says Cofounder Kip Tindell. "Each VP spends 30 to 45 minutes updating the other VPs on their areas. We review the profit and loss statement, and everything that is going on in the business at that point in time is discussed in detail." Copious notes are taken, and each VP then takes the information and meets with their people. From there, information is trickled down so that everyone is informed. "We are really, really big on everyone participating in that information. I want the part-time cashier, if interested, to have the ability to know the expansion policies, the financial performance, and everything but salaries. We don't talk about individual salaries—but just about everything else, because then you are really interested and really excited and then you are really empowered and can really care as opposed to playing some kind of game where you don't know what the score is." All information is eventually put into reports that are shared with everyone—even information from staff meetings. "I know occasionally it falls into the wrong hands of the competitor, and that is painful, because everything is discussed and the notes are not edited," Tindell says. But, he adds, he and the other Cofounder, Garrett Boone, decided a long time ago that it was more important to, "be willing to spend a lot more money on getting that information, than it is to worry about the negative ramifications of the information occasionally falling in the wrong hands. You can't have a team that way. You can't have communication that way. It's invigorating to be involved. It is so easy to get people to act in concert and harmony with each other once they are all given the same set of information."

Boone and Tindell are willing to take the risk because they say it works. "It's our nature I guess," says Boone. "That's the kind of environment that we like and the people we've hired like that too. If there's stuff you don't know anything about, you can't represent the company. If you knew information was being withheld, you wouldn't want to represent the company." They simply do what seems to be right.

True leaders go to great lengths to keep their people informed. Regardless of the size of the organization, leaders agree that information flow strengthens everyone's understanding and helps individuals to see the important role they each contribute to the company's overall success. When this happens, true teamwork prevails.

EXPLORE AND DISCOVER

- How do you rate yourself as an effective listener?

- Whom do you tend to listen to the most?

- How often do you take time to listen to people in other departments of the company or people in similar roles within other industries?

- How well do you use open-ended questions to probe?

- How do you feel when you know someone has really listened to you?

- How do you ensure that your information flows to everyone involved?

- What could you do to strengthen your communication skills?

- How well do you communicate via e-mail?

- Do you ever abuse the use of e-mail?

- Do you use voice mail or e-mail to avoid, or do you always use it appropriately?

- How does your voice mail message sound? Would you like to do business with you?

- How well do you use the gift of feedback?

- Do you post quotes to help motivate you?

- Could "quote corners" help to motivate and inspire in your organization?

5

PRINCIPLE FOUR

Treat Learning
Like Dirty Dishes

True leaders never stop learning. Weight Watchers President and CEO Linda Huett says learning is like dirty dishes—you never finish in terms of your own development. "No matter what you're appointed, you are still just learning, and you've got as much to learn from the people who work for you as you've got to give them," she says. "By the same token, being able to make decisions and being decisive, and how you can move from where you are now to where you want the company to be, is the single most important trait that you can bring to your leadership role."

True leaders are humble enough to realize they don't know it all. They engage their people purposefully at all levels, knowing that often the distance between the front line and the senior leadership team may be so great that one small piece of information may have tremendous impact. True leaders learn from a variety of sources. They are avid readers of books; they listen to audiotapes; they seek out advice from experts, peers, and mentors; and they even resort to sage advise given by parents. They embrace a process of self-discovery and view most mistakes as learning experiences. They learn from young, new thinkers as well as from those who are more seasoned and experienced. They even glean powerful lessons from bad examples.

A never-to-be-forgotten moment that had dramatic impact on Jack Kahl's life happened in 1973, two years after he had bought Manco. "I was 32 years old and I was sitting at home alone, watching the third leg of the Belmont race. Secretariat had won the first two legs and was going for the Triple Crown. I'd never been to a horse race at that point, but as a kid I had worked in a stable running horses and cleaning the stables. I had read every book on stallions and I always loved the story of this wild stallion that couldn't be tamed. I think I always associated that with me, and how I wanted to be free to be who I wanted to be. In any case, Secretariat won the race in world-record time and won the Triple Crown." Suddenly Kahl found himself sitting there, all by himself, crying—absolutely sobbing. What was going through Kahl's mind was the power of competing against no one but himself—just as the horse had done. "From this day forward, I can only compare myself to myself," Kahl found himself thinking. "No more comparisons to other people. I'll be as good as I can be, proven by me, for me." Kahl recalls the incident as one of the best moments of his life because after that, "I became a total student of everything. I loved learning with a passion that I never had in school. You might say a horse changed my life."

Three years later, Kahl had the opportunity to meet Sam Walton, the founder of Wal-Mart, a company with which Kahl was developing a business relationship. About the third time they met, Jack was carrying a book. He handed it to Sam. "Sam looked me in the eye and said, 'You're a real student of management, aren't you, Jack?' I said, 'Yes, sir, I am.' 'So am I,' he said. 'I'll make you a deal. If you share with me the best things you read and learn, I'll do the same with you.'" That momentary exchange turned into a lifetime friendship based not just on learning, but on loving to learn together. "Our bond grew these big stacks of letters that were all about learning together," Kahl said. "Listen, learn, lead; listen, learn, lead. Basic stuff. At home I have two leather-bound books—each of them several inches high—of letters from Sam that we shared because of our loving to learn together. Sam Walton, who is sort of the divining rod of my life for business, is by far the seminal leader." Kahl recalled that Sam told him most of what he learned he took from other people's books. It was not new—what he did was amalgamate it together and make it his. "Then," Kahl said, "he put a cheer around the front and back of it. When you are talking to me about leadership, you will hear me tell you the Wal-Mart story because it became the Manco story. I built my business as an altar boy to serve the customer." This is a strategy Kahl learned firsthand from Sam Walton. From 1976 to 1988, Kahl continued to learn from Walton. This learning worked so well that it helped Kahl grow his little company into a multi-million dollar business that has now become global.

LEARNING FROM PARENTS, PEERS, AND MENTORS

David Novak says he never started his career by thinking he would become CEO of a company. "But I think what allowed me to get to that point is that you see other people that you have respect for as individuals, and at the same time you recognize that they don't have anything that you don't necessarily have. So I think your eyes open up to your possibilities as you grow up and you get exposed to things and meet really good people." The Tricon Chairman and CEO attributes his self-esteem for thinking he could eventually be a leader to his mother. "I grew up in a tremendous family. It was lower middle class. My father was a surveyor for the government. We lived in a trailer, and I lived in 23 states by the time I was in eighth grade. When you move three times a year, you have to make friends. My mother would say, 'You have three or four months to make some friends. If you don't take the initiative, you're not going to have any friends.'" Novak's parents also gave him the opportunity to go to college. "My parents wanted more for me then they had for themselves. I was the first one in the family to get a college education. I never forget that my mom and dad have all the talent that I have, they just didn't get the opportunity. They didn't have the money to get a college education at the time, they didn't have the mentor to push them, but given the right kind of circumstances, I'm absolutely convinced that my parents could have achieved very high levels in any company. So I think it [leadership] starts with parents and the environment they set."

Novak says that every person he has ever worked for has invested in him and he in them. "I think that you cannot underestimate how important it is to work for a leader who invests in your career." Novak says the best advice he will give to his daughter, who is about to begin college, is to make sure that she likes whoever she goes to work for. "Be sure that you can learn from them and that they are going to invest in you, and you see them growing in the company. Because the worst thing that you can do is to get sidetracked by somebody that isn't going to invest in you and that isn't a leader." Novak says that in his own career, he has been able to learn from watching many different styles and many different approaches. "I'm a learner," he says. "You don't have to know everything if you can learn from others."

Novak also believes you are a product of what you are exposed to. "If you stay among the same group of friends or the same company without getting outside of your industry, you will become very limited in your thinking." Novak reads everything he can about leadership. When we interviewed him, he was on his way to Austin, Texas, taking his team to a technology company. "We're meeting with the executive team, and we're going to talk about the Internet and how you can apply it to motivating and inspiring and communicating with employees," Novak explained. "I don't know if we'll do any of that stuff, but we're going to go there and get outside of ourselves for about four or five hours as an executive team, and we'll get some different exposure." He says that what he loves most is building the capabilities of his leadership team and making sure that he always shares what he, himself, learns.

"How many people get a chance to meet with Jack Welch?" he asks. Now, I can keep that conversation to myself, or I can share what I've learned." Novak says he also got a chance to spend one and one half hours with Warren Buffett. He took copious notes that have become a two-page learning primer from Buffett. "I share this with the finance people, and I build it into my leadership program. I get to meet people—do things, go places—that most people will never ever get to do. So I think what I need to do is share it—not just keep it for myself—to give credit where credit is due."

Learn from the Experienced

As AICP CEO, Tim Webster learns from a board chairman within a corporate setup that is more common in Europe than it is in the United States. "We have a nonexecutive chairman who retired from the Kellogg Company in 1989. He lives on Hilton Head Island and spends two to three days a month with us, primarily mentoring me and the top management group and assisting us in creating the vision for the company. He has been a great mentor in terms of teaching me the ins and outs of running a food company. After 30 years with Kellogg, he has incredible depth of knowledge and experience and a mastery of so many disciplines that I have benefited greatly from that." Webster thinks the structure of having the Chairman and the CEO separated to have a true check and balance, as opposed to the common rubber stamp board of directors, is a very good idea. "Particularly as people live longer," he points out. "These folks finish their careers at age 65 and still have many, many more years to give. As we become more comfortable with the idea of mentoring and coaching and teaching, I think this will be catching on more and more."

Webster believes that when you have a setup with the Chairman/CEO and a hand-selected board, the CEO doesn't get much true feedback. "Honest, constructive feedback for the CEO, as we have in this environment, is very unique. It's a good model," says Webster. This model provides him a wisdom and insight that many of his peers might envy.

Dan Woodward is another CEO who has drawn from experience. He hired Jack Mullinax to be CFO and Executive Vice President. Mullinax is a 30-plus-year business leader who was once Woodward's boss's boss. "This is my third opportunity to work with Jack," Woodward says. "I first worked in Jack's organization as a young financial analyst when I joined IBM. He made such an impression on me that I always looked for opportunities to work with him." Several years ago, Mullinax led the Human Resources department of a joint venture headed up by Woodward prior to his joining Enherent. "After I came here, I lured him out of IBM and got him to hold off on retirement for a couple of years to help me." Woodward calls seasoned veterans of industry his secret weapons. "The thing I've learned is I can communicate with them quickly and they understand me—how I operate, how I communicate, and what I want to get done and how. And they are willing to challenge me. They can say, 'You're an idiot, why would you want to do that?'" Woodward credits Mullinax for having had more aggregate impact on him over the years than anyone. And the role reversal seems to work very well. "It's never been a problem for me to have those roles reversed," said Mullinax. "I feel like, today, he and I are partners in this venture. He creates that kind of environment where it is a partnership." Mullinax has also observed Woodward's learning and maturing. "In the past, a long time ago, Dan would have been right in the middle of conflict. He was a very courageous young man who would not have backed away from anything. But, today, he's able to see the larger picture and recognize that there are some things you just have to let go and move on. He was always very consumed by his work, and that hasn't changed. But as you take on a greater role of responsibility, you realize that there are clearly just some things that you don't have time to do—that you have to delegate. I've seen him learn to release things. He can release them and truly feel okay delegating." One of the areas that Mullinax says Woodward has brought to the organization that helps even the senior team continue to learn is to evaluate each of the leaders on leadership attributes. "In the first evaluation that he did of me last year, it was the first time I had seen that, and I thought it was a nice touch," Mullinax said. "He evaluates us based on how he sees us in those attributes, and in doing so, he encourages us to embrace those attributes that he values." Woodward was happy to share the unique evaluation for any leader to adapt or build upon. (A copy of Wodward's evaluation form can be found in Appendix C.)

Learn from Great Bosses

Sometimes it's just the little things that stick the most. Feedback Plus CEO Vicki Henry recalls one trait she learned from her first boss—a bank president. "I don't care how busy the man was and I don't care how hard he worked, you could walk into his office and ask for a minute and he would say 'two' and hold up two fingers. Years later, when somebody walked into my office and asked to have a minute, I said 'two' and held up two fingers. It's like I had just mirrored something I had always loved in him, because you always knew you could talk to him. He always had time for you, but he always told you how much time." Henry says that because time management was a lesson she had to learn, she learned a good one from her boss.

Bill Matthews learned many powerful lessons from Plante & Moran's cofounder, Frank Moran. One such lesson was a story the late Moran shared with him about a student who had come to visit the office. A staff person had taken the student to meet a partner, but the partner was on the phone, so he covered up the mouthpiece, and said, "I'm busy right now, take him to somebody else and I'll talk to him later." The staff person complied. As they left the office and walked down the hall, they ran into Frank Moran who asked the student how things were going. "Oh, pretty well," he replied, "except that I just had to rearrange an office visit." Moran asked why. The student told him what had just transpired. So Moran walked down to the partner's office, went in, and the partner said to the person on the phone, "I'll have to call you back," and hung up. "Why did you do that?" Moran asked. "Well, because you came in to talk with me," the partner responded. "Didn't a student come in to talk with you?" Moran asked. The partner affirmed that he had. "So," asked Moran, "what do you think you should have done when the student walked in?" The partner acknowledged that he should have done the same thing he had done when Moran walked in. "And what do you think you ought to do now?" Moran asked. "Well, I ought to go get him," the partner said. Moran agreed.

Moran's story made such a powerful point. "We all get caught up in what we are doing, and it is okay to remind somebody that maybe they could have made a different choice," Matthews said, pointing out that everyone has a level of importance—not just the boss.

Irv Hockaday says he was mentored by a wonderful character named Bill Deramus. He was the Chairman of Kansas City Southern Industries and hired Hockaday prior to his going to Hallmark. "He knew better, but he acted like he thought you could do anything," Hockaday recalled. "He didn't give you a lot of guidance, although if you went in and asked him, he might give you some help. He usually said, 'Why don't you figure that out?' But, if you went out and botched it up and the Board of Directors wanted to know how in the heck we got in this situation, Bill always assumed responsibility for it. He was a mentor in the sense that he let you spread your wings."

Gary Nelon learned from his early boss, the President of Austin National Bank, that balancing the human factor with the financial factor was very important. "Austin Stone is one of the finest human beings I have ever known. He's 87 now," said Nelon. "The model that he gave me in a pretty good-sized organization was that you can have a successful enterprise but still have a sense of family about that enterprise. If everybody understands what the role of the individuals working in the company is, you can accomplish things together if you are communicating well enough what the lay of the land is. He had a great track record of earnings for a long period of time. But, above all things, he was a great human being."

Learn from Bad Bosses

Ann Hambly says she had a lot of reverse mentoring. "I've had a few bosses that treated me in such a way that I will never, ever treat an employee like that," says Hambly. "I had one who was extremely verbally abusive, and she would frequently talk down to you and you would feel just horrible. I thought, there is no reason, no benefit, to treat people like that." Hambly learned from this negative experience and made a promise to herself that she would never be that kind of a boss.

When we asked Jim Copeland about mentors, there was a long pause, then a hearty laugh. "I had a number of what I would call negative examples of leadership," he confessed. "I always said you could learn from anybody you worked for. You either learned what you wanted to emulate or you learned that you didn't want to emulate them." Copeland says it's funny how the negative examples stick with you. "I remember we had a managing partner who said if you have over ten hours of overtime, you have to have it approved before you work it. We were in the midst of this busy season, and a manager that was working on one of my jobs was going to go beyond the 50 hours allocated, and it was a Saturday or Sunday night before we figured that out. So I told him to go ahead and work the hours. The managing partner the next day asked why he worked the extra hours that weren't authorized. I told him we didn't realize we were going to work them until it was midnight on Saturday night and I didn't think he'd appreciate a phone call. The partner said, 'Well, we're not going to pay him for the hours.' I said, 'Well, you're confused about who's in charge here. The talented people are the ones in charge. The only people that we can order around and treat as if they don't have any options are those people who don't have any options. They are not the people we want to keep in the organization.' It was just a classic example of somebody absolutely determined to have his will obeyed no matter whether it happened to make sense to the circumstances or not. It was just absolutely stupid."

LEARN FROM YOUR OWN WEAKNESSES

Terri Bowersock not only learned about business from peer members of her leadership team, she learned an important lesson about herself. As part of Bowersock's growth after starting her consign and design business, she realized that she needed to hire several people more highly educated than herself. So she brought on a CEO and CFO—people she now refers to as her C's. Soon the C's started making decisions that Bowersock saw as dramatic changes. "At first, I really fought with them," she recalled. "Then one day, I stopped fighting and I could see that they were smarter. Then I got very withdrawn and insecure about it. I thought, how am I ever going to be a leader again? How am I ever going to step back into that position?" Then she rationalized that it was okay—it wasn't important for her to know all the nuts and bolts. But she still saw things that were not congruent with the vision she had about the consignment business. "For example, I knew that you can get 14 pick-ups in a day, but it's not worth it. Your body hurts, it's hot and 110 degrees in Phoenix, and it just not worth it past eight pick-ups." There were things that looked good on paper to the C's that Bowersock knew were not the same when actually doing it. So the changes began to frustrate her. Then a friend pointed out something important to her one day. "You know, these people can come in and do this job because you have already built something," the friend said. "But these people probably could not have started how you started—with nothing but a hope and a dream. They know how to come in and do nuts and bolts, but you have to remember that they may never have been able to come in and start the company." Bowersock said that at that moment she was able to step back and realize, "I'm a founder. For the nuts and bolts, the smartest thing you can do is to hire someone smarter than yourself. So I stepped back and said, my job is just to say thank you." From that day forward, she took back her leadership role of strategically planning the growth of the business as she, and only she, knows it. "We're not here to be a new furniture store—we're a consignment store. That's my job as a leader—I have to keep Terri's what it is even though the big guys come along with lots of big degrees, convinced that their way is right. I have to have the gumption to keep coming in and saying, here's what I intuitively think." Today Bowersock jokes about her lack of education and the fact that she doesn't have a business degree. "What I do have is a BMW degree," she says with a laugh. "That's because in my car [a BMW, of course] I'm never without a cassette. I love entrepreneurial stories, and I am just constantly listening to stories about entrepreneurs." That's how Bowersock continues to learn. Plus, as a dyslexic, she has found that other dyslexic people have had a profound effect on her. "I had always hidden that I was dyslexic and felt very shamed about it until I found out that Albert Einstein, Thomas Edison, John F. Kennedy, and Walt Disney were all dyslexic. I went, 'Wow, if they can be, I can be.'" So they, too, have become her role model mentors.

Learn from Mistakes

Linda Huett believes that people at every level will try to hide mistakes as if they didn't happen. Or they will try to find something external to explain that it had nothing to do with them or their organization. "The first thing a leader has to do is to have people face reality," Huett says. "Accept responsibility and admit that we did make the mistake, or our team made the mistake, or that we could have done something better and therefore investigating that will help us not to make a similar mistake in the future." Huett says people far too often look for scapegoats so everybody can point to the mistake being someone else's fault. "Usually it isn't any one individual's fault anyway," she says. "So talking about mistakes is the first thing. We all make mistakes. We try not to have them, and we certainly don't do them intentionally." Living up to the mistake and learning from it is what's really important.

Mike McCarthy owned up to a big mistake several years ago that taught him a very hard lesson. "We built the company up and it got too big. I wasn't watching it as I should have been, and we lost $22 million in one year," he confessed. "The bonding company quit us, the banks quit us, and everyone tried to hold us up." It was an incredibly difficult time for McCarthy, but he didn't shirk his leadership responsibilities. "I drove around the country with my wife and two little babies in a Dodge minivan and a trailer for our clothes. I personally went and laid every person off. The reason I did this was because I had screwed it up. They had done their jobs, I hadn't done mine, but they were going to lose their jobs while I got to keep mine.

"I wanted to have the pain of doing that so I would never ever forget. It was rugged. But to a person, they all really appreciated it [his telling them himself]." That was in the mid-1980s. McCarthy has since restructured the building company, and it is now stronger than ever—ranking among the nation's top ten commercial construction companies. And many of the people he had to lay off have returned. It was a major mistake, but also a major learning experience.

Learn from Humility

"I think one of my great assets is knowing what I don't know—what I'm not good at," says Irv Hockaday. "I don't know if that is realism or humility, but it's certainly important." Gary McDaniel simply says, "Don't take yourself too seriously." He believes that many times in a leadership position, ego tends to get in the way. "When you do that," he says, "the balance of the organization suffers." McDaniel shares a story that he learned early in his career when he was a second lieutenant in the Air Force that demonstrates the point. "I was at an assignment and had a fellow working for me that was a Chief Master Sergeant. I had been in this job and had worked with him for about a year and a half, and it was time for me to get transferred to another assignment. I was bemoaning the situation and saying, 'Gosh, I'm so good, who's going to come and take my place—how can anybody do this just as good as me?'" The Chief Master Sergeant looked at McDaniel and said, "Lieutenant, if you pull your arm out of a bucket of water, how long does the hole last?" McDaniel said, "I've taken that with me for the past 30 years or so. It's a very true statement—the hole doesn't last very long." Neither do leaders with self-inflated egos.

So, like dirty dishes, learning is never finished for true leaders. Their commitment to continual learning is one principle that separates them from the rest.

EXPLORE AND DISCOVER

- What are your plans for continual learning?

- Who are your mentors?

- Whom do you mentor—formally or informally?

- How can you learn from other leaders in your organization?

- What do you do to demonstrate your commitment to lifelong learning?

- How humble are you?

- How do you handle mistakes?

- How do you deal with your own mistakes?

- What role did your parents play in your leadership learning?

- From whom have you learned something very valuable that you would least expect to learn from?

- What do you do to share what you have learned?

6 PRINCIPLE FIVE

Do What's Right and Tell the Truth

Popularity rarely has much to do with true leadership. While true leaders generally inspire a strong following, they can stand firm on difficult decisions that may be unpopular at the time yet, in truth, are best for the organization in the long run. David Walker was in the midst of just such an issue when we interviewed him. Since November 1998, as the Comptroller General of the United States, Walker has been forging major changes at the General Accounting Office—some of which have not been very popular—particularly his revamping of the agency's performance system.

"Right now we have a performance system, which many employers have in the private sector, that suffers from grade inflation and a lack of meaningful dispersion in the ratings. We have to be more honest with each other about how people are really performing as compared to standards, and we need to let them know where they stand over their peers."

Walker says he's had a lot of "push back" on the changes he's trying to make. "People say, 'Oh, we can't do that, it's going to demotivate people.'" Walker disagrees. "It's called honesty," he says. "I am not going to apologize for honesty. That's part of being principled. How we do it, I can be flexible on. Whether we do it, I'm not."

Having a set of principles to consistently apply—being fair, open, and honest—has been at the forefront of Walker's drive for change, and he unquestioningly believes the changes are the right thing to do. His attitude reflects the principles of one of his political role models—former President Teddy Roosevelt. "He was a true leader," Walker said. "He said what he meant and meant what he said. One of the biggest things about him was he was very principled. He fought for what he thought was right and didn't do things based on a poll or popular opinion." Walker is taking the same approach. He says that both in the private sector and in the government, a lack of effective communication exists between supervisors and managers and their employees with regard to expectations, and meaningful feedback on individual strengths, as well as areas where individuals are not as strong. "You see that in performance appraisal systems, including ours that we are scrapping. We are fundamentally going to a new one because the old one is not giving us what we need." Walker believes a performance system needs to accomplish several things: identify people's strengths and weaknesses so everybody can get honest feedback and help; give you enough information so that you can recognize and reward top performers; and provide enough information so that you can deal with nonperformers.

"Going back to trust," Walker says, "any major decision that is going to have a major impact on our people and how they do business or their work environment, we will post it and allow all our employees to comment on it. We will do this after we come up with a proposal, because otherwise it is not manageable. The idea is to avoid surprises and allow everyone to participate. Not everybody is going to agree, but a vast majority will, and at least they will have the opportunity to be heard." From Walker's perspective, he is doing what's right because the new system will provide more truthful information. "Without that information, you are in the dark, and that's not right for you and it's not right for the organization."

Walker isn't alone in taking a stand. Many of the leaders we interviewed believe that telling the truth removes doubt and emphasizes accountability.

TELL THE TRUTH ABOUT REORGANIZATIONS, LAYOFFS, AND FIRING

Len Roberts says that when he took over his leadership role at Radio Shack, some people were worried about the changes he would make and whether they would be with the organization the following year. "I don't know if it's going to be a single change, or if no one's going to be in this room next year and it will be different people," he told managers during his introduction speech. "I'm not interested in who got the results," Roberts told them. "I want to know who got results and developed their people at the same time." He says, "Lots of folks were getting results but were hurting people in the process." So Roberts let people know the truth right from the start—results were important, but not at the cost of people. Teamwork was important, too. "I think we're all members of a team," Roberts explained. "I've always preached this. I'll give anyone the benefit of the doubt, but if they're hurting people or they're destructive, or they are trying to destroy the team spirit, I'm like a laser. I'm not impulsive, but once I have made that conclusion, they're just gone—they're just out. I preach that. I hate summarily firing people. I always want to give people the benefit. But, if ever I draw the conclusion that somebody's out there trying to destroy the team, I remove them surgically—quickly and fast."

When a company needs to restructure, David Novak says the most important thing is to explain why. "People need to know why you're restructuring," says the Tricon Chairman. "Is it because the company has to restructure to be successful for the long term? If you're one of the people who won't have a job, there's not a whole lot you can do to make that person feel better. But the most dignity you can give it is to at least let people know why it is happening. I think that's treating people with respect."

True leaders know that reorganizations, layoffs, and firings are realities of business cycles. Jim Copeland believes you can go through a downsizing exercise or fire people, but you have to do it in a way that doesn't violate the trust of the organization. "One recession, we had the unfortunate experience of being overstaffed versus the economies that we had," said the Deloitte & Touche CEO. "We had that problem in the practice unit that I was leading at the time. We sent a message that said, 'This is where we are, this is what we're going to have to do. We don't want to do it, but we are caught in circumstances where we have no real choice. At the same time we want to do this in a way that doesn't violate our relationships and our culture. So we're going to hold ourselves accountable to you until we have every one of these people placed in a job, and we will report back to you.' We were religious about doing that. So you can do hard things in difficult circumstances, but you have to do them in a way that doesn't violate the trust."

Juxtapose Copeland's philosophy with the manner in which Dell Computer Corporation cut its workforce. *Time* magazine reported details of the brutal scenario where members of the firing squad didn't even introduce themselves and avoided eye contact by standing with their backs to people as they came in. They took a mere eight minutes to tell 1,700 people they were no longer needed, and officers from the Texas Department of Public Safety were on hand to escort fired workers to their cars. CEO Michael Dell reportedly told the magazine that they tried to handle the layoffs humanely. He reportedly felt beat up by the media. Well, Dell may not have been the one in the room, but as the ultimate leader, he allowed the process to be handled in a manner anything but humane. You be the judge. Would you consider Jim Copeland, or Michael Dell, to be the true leader?

True leadership starts at the top, and incongruent actions that seemingly are condoned by the top leader send a message much louder than any words. Copeland says, "I don't think talking about the organization being trustworthy is particularly effective or helpful. I think people look a lot at the people you promote and put in leadership roles, and that is what communicates." Copeland says that if the people see that you are putting individuals in those roles whom they respect and trust and whose values support the espoused values and philosophies of the organization, they attribute that to consistency and a quality organization. If not, employees get a very different message.

TELL THE TRUTH FOR ACCOUNTABILITY

Jim Nicholson says that through the years, he has learned hard work, honesty, and integrity. He has also learned that it's important to be polite, but firm. "Polite but firm is, you are running one of my operations—a $20 million business—and it's not going well. We've agreed that you're going to make a million dollars on this business, but you're losing a million dollars. What do I do about that? I could have you in a public meeting and have a temper tantrum, yell and scream at you and tell you that you're a worthless human being and that I should have never given you the job, and you're fired. Or I could have a private meeting and tell you that you're a fine person but this is not working out and ask what you are going to do to fix it in the next 30 days. You don't have to shout, you don't have to scream, but you do need to be firm and clear. I think it's about having expectations for people that are clearly communicated, but then they are held accountable for them in a kind, but firm, way. In other words, in this case, it isn't going to be 31 days. It's going to be better in 30 days, or you're going to be doing something else."

The PVS President says it's also important to tell the truth and take action if a member of the leadership team operates in a style that is inconsistent with the values that have been established for the work environment. "If I buy a company and I find that the leadership is inconsistent with our views, I replace that leadership." Nicholson cites this example: "I bought a company that had 400 people, and the organization chart was the leader and 400 people. He was the only one who made any decisions about anything, and if you made any other decisions, you suffered. I replaced him, at some economic cost, because there was nobody in place to replace him. So the employees wandered in the wilderness, not for 40 years, but for 4 months. But I wouldn't allow that kind of dictatorial, nonparticipatory style. I really do feel that folks I work with are my people and I have a responsibility to them. I don't want them mistreated."

TELL THE TRUTH TO BEGIN WITH

The day Bruce Simpson took over as CEO of AppGenesys, he made a welcome speech to all the people. "I said something to the effect of, you may not always like what I have to say, but what I say will be consistent and always the truth. I don't hide things. There are no secrets. If there is something that I can't share with you, I will tell you why I can't share it with you. Sometimes I sign nondisclosure agreements or I'm dealing with public information, or I have information that legally I can't share. In that case, if there's something that you ask me that I can't share with you, I'll give you a reason why." Simpson says it's important to impress upon people that information is powerful, but only if everybody has it. "When people lack information, they tend to fill in those gaps anyway, and what they tend to fill them in with is often the wrong, negative stuff." Telling the truth helps to avoid a misinformed workforce and ward off false rumors.

The other thing Simpson thinks is important to tell the truth about is that no such thing as job security exists. Simpson told his people from the start, "I'm sorry, there is no job security. Just get that out of your head. The only security anybody has in life is to make sure that the business stays healthy. So if we work together and do the things that we are talking about to build a healthy, vibrant business, it provides an environment for us to have healthy, vibrant careers. But, even in sight of all of that, it is still our responsibility to make sure that our skills have stayed well aligned with the business—our skills have to continue to develop." Telling the truth sets the expectations straight to begin with.

TELL THE TRUTH TO ENSURE THE RIGHT FIT

Ann Hambly admits that her core personality is to be a pleaser. "I like to try to make everybody happy," she says, "and I would love to do that." But in her leadership role at Prudential Asset Resources, she realizes that is not always possible, and even if you try, it sometimes hurts people in the long run. "What I had to learn early on is what people expect more than anything else out of the leader is honesty. Treat them as adults and communicate. Sometimes the message is not a fun message, but you have to deliver it. The worst thing you can do to people in the interest of trying to keep them happy, is to not tell them the truth." When it comes to promoting people, Hambly thinks what companies typically do is look at all the workers and decide that one of them does excellent work. That's the person they pick to be the next leader. "They take that person who is really good and put him up here as a manager of people. A lot of people don't stop to see if that person has the inherent, core, basic traits of what it would take to be a manger, let alone a leader. There are a lot of people in companies who are around me all the time that got there because they were really good at what they did, but they're not really good at being a manager. So there are lots of companies filled with people who are just really good workers who got to the top because of that." Hambly says both are needed. But if she has someone who is a really good worker but does not have the core people skills that it takes to be a good leader, and she has someone else who is a little less effi-cient at getting the work done but has the core people skills, she will pick the less tactical person. "A lot of times if you ask a per-son, they don't really want to be a manager—they just want to do their job. I like those people, they're wonderful—they are the organization."

Hambly says that too often, the better a person is with tech-nical skills, the more they are going to move ahead. According to Hambly, that's not dealing truthfully with the individual. "You end up with people who don't know how to manage people. These are typically people that don't delegate because they still want to do things. I've worked with managers who have a slew of skills that aren't necessary to their job, and a lot of the skills that they need, they don't have."

Most leaders agree that soft skills rather than technical skills become more critical as one ascends into higher leadership roles. Yet soft skills often are not an integral part of the organization's training budget, thus contributing to the many wrong-fit promo-tions that Hambly talks about.

TELL THE TRUTH ABOUT CAPABILITIES

"I have to be honest with you," Dr. Alvin Rohrs says about hiring people. "I have learned over the years to recognize fairly early if there isn't a real fit. As an example, we've got 20 projects going on at the same time, and if you're not good at juggling, you're going to be miserable in my office. If I recognize that early, I can sit down with somebody and say, 'You're not having fun here. I think your life would be better off if you went somewhere else and found another position. We'll try to help you do that, but this just isn't the kind of place you want to be working and we recognize that.'" Rohrs says that if you can get these people out of the organization quickly enough, you can still part friends. "You don't wait until they blow some really big project because they couldn't handle the pressure." The CEO of SIFE admits to trying historically to carry people too long, even when he knew in his heart that the person was never going to enjoy working in the organization and was never going to get their job done. "I used to think the worst thing you could do was to fire somebody, and I hate to do that. But you are really doing them a favor by telling them the truth." Often, helping the person move to the right job with the right environment for their personality and capabilities is doing them a favor.

Linda Huett believes it is part of every manager's responsibility to talk about their individual team member's traits in a truthful manner. "That's a very difficult thing to do for a lot of managers," the Weight Watchers CEO says. "Learning how to talk about the difficult things with an individual person within your team is one of the skills you have to learn very early on to become effective. If you have too many players on your team that are just not playing, then your team won't function," she cautions. Huett doesn't like the word *weaknesses*. She prefers to talk in terms of *traits*. She says you can see all parts of you and your management and the way you do things as traits. Some traits taken to extremes can actually be a handicap to the team. "If we take something like attention to detail," she says, "that's just a trait. You have either a poor attention to detail—you don't notice the detail and you're not concerned with the detail, therefore if it is taken to a real extreme, you can get very sloppy, slap-dash, and you won't be as effective as you could if you paid more attention to the detail. Or there's the other extreme, where you can have people that are so fanatical about the detail that they are—in the old cliché—missing the forest for the trees. They're looking at every leaf, and therefore they are not able to maximize what can be done because of all those little details that slow them down and distract them from getting the whole thing done." Huett says it is the leader's or manager's responsibility to discuss truthfully the extreme of these kinds of traits as it relates to maximizing the individual's effectiveness.

TELL THE TRUTH TO ELIMINATE FATAL ERRORS

Vicki Henry remembers reading a book several years ago about fatal errors that managers make. One was condoning incompetence. "I always thought that anybody could do anything if they had the right environment and the right coaching," Henry professed. "Well, that ain't so. If someone is truly inefficient and continues to make mistakes that affect your product or your customer service, then I think you have to learn to eliminate those mistakes." If that means being truthful and eliminating the person, then that needs to be done, says the CEO of Feedback Plus. "If it's an attitude problem, I think not only should you eliminate it, but you should do so quickly and consider it like a cancer. There are probably other people around that person that need to be cut out as well. I've had to go through that a number of times at my company, and it's not fun." It is facing up to the truth, however.

TELL THE TRUTH TO DEMONSTRATE AUTHENTICITY

Dan Woodward thinks most people don't expect CEOs to be real, honest, and open and to really care and have emotion. But he says, "Being real works." Woodward tells of a time before joining Enherent when he personally learned from a leader that it was okay to be real. "The executive vice president of corporate services for IBM was coming in, and everybody was busy with arrangements. My boss said, 'I'll pick him up in my pickup truck, and he can throw his coffee cup in the back just like I do.' That's when I realized that you could be an executive and be a real person too. I think it's important for people to recognize that and to understand that there are certain things that come with position, but when it's all said and done, executives are just people and everyone needs to recognize that they have a human side too—that there is a human being behind that role."

THE TRUTH HELPS TO ESTABLISH LIMITS

Tim Webster believes a leader can be seen as a good guy, but not as a pushover. "My boss has a saying: If you present yourself as a pancake, you'll be eaten like a pancake." Webster says the statement is based on the principle that emotions have limits. As an example, the President and CEO of American Italian Pasta Co. says it is important to hold to your own truths with customers to be sure that while you may be a nice guy, you do have defined limits. "I think a lot of times customers will see where your limits are. They will ask for and take until you say, wait a minute. So I think if you present yourself like a pancake, you'll be eaten like a pancake." Webster points out that while he finds it important, as a leader, to see that customer needs are met, he finds it equally important to meet the needs of his people and to ensure that his suppliers are dealt with in a tough, but fair, way that is sustainable, and that the company also delivers something good for its shareholders. "I can always rob my people and my suppliers to be better to my customers. But, if that gets out of balance, then it is not a sustainable ecosystem," Webster points out.

To Webster, telling the truth in business relates to business principles and moral integrity. "We believe that we have to conduct our business in a legal and responsible manner, so there are external forces that you have to operate within—whether it is tax law or FDA or EPA—that is the most simplistic external definition. Then we have a set of values that we like to conduct ourselves with that are part of our mission statement. We want to be open and involve our people. We want to be consistent and prudent in our marketplace strategies. And we want to compete aggressively within those limits and parameters and work proactively—anticipating, as opposed to reacting. We like to promote from within whenever possible, because our belief is that the best people are already inside the company. So we want to grow and develop our people. We want to pay them a fair wage, and it is heavily skewed toward performance and incentive based so that we have a performance-based culture. And we want to deal with nonperformers in an open, fair, and reasonable fashion."

These truths are the truths upon which Webster's corporate culture is built. When it comes to determining who fits their culture and who doesn't, he likes to be truthful and honest about that too. "Before it was taboo to talk about the fact that certain people don't fit in your culture. I like to say we can only have 500 people here. It should be a privilege to work on this team. We should hold each other to high standards and expect a lot from each other and from ourselves. We have a pretty rich fabric of what our principles and values are, and I think you'd find that they are well understood in our organization." As a result, the company is selective about whom they hire, and they are very direct about their expectation of doing what's right and telling the truth.

True leaders have a high regard for integrity, honesty, and doing what's right, which all begins with being committed to telling the truth.

EXPLORE AND DISCOVER

- How committed are you to always telling the truth?

- How easy would it be for you to inform an employee that they were not the right fit for a specific position?

- What situations cause you the most difficulty when telling the truth?

- What would you consider the right thing to do if you had to lay off hundreds of people?

- What process do you have in place to ensure that when you hire, you hire the right fit?

- When is the last time you told the truth about a difficult decision?

- How well do you take the truth regarding your own performance review?

- Have you ever promoted someone into management who lacked the appropriate people skills?

- Have you evaluated your own strengths and weaknesses?

- Do you spend most of your time developing your strengths or your weaknesses?

7

Trust Is a Must

Trust is the basis from which all true leaders operate. Without trust, there is little on which to build sustainable success. And, while it may seem trite to say this, so much erosion of trust has occurred in business over the past few years, that our economy has suffered consequences. In a business world that has become global in scope and rapid in pace, any hint of distrust can quickly deteriorate the relationships essential to building long-term, sustainable success. Leaders who adhere to the principle that trust is a must and demonstrate it through trust-building actions will be the ones to reap long-term success.

Jim Copeland remembers hearing the great football coach, Lou Holtz, talk about principles of leadership. "Can I trust you? Do you care about me as a person? Are you committed to excellence? If you can answer those three questions positively, the rest of the things will fall into place," Copeland recalled. "I really believe that. I think those are the right issues to focus on. Everything else you do is ineffective if people don't trust you. Second," he says, "they have to believe. It really helps if they believe that the leaders in the organization actually care about what happens to their people. Third is about excellence. I think one of the oldest motivating factors in history around work has been the quality of work. Most people want to be the best at what they do." These are three principles that Copeland has used over and over as foundations of his leadership.

True leaders agree that establishing an open environment is one of the first requirements for building an environment of trust. People need to believe that they can freely express their thoughts and be taken seriously. Copeland also believes that it does little good merely to talk about trust. "I think they have to see it in action," he says. "People have to understand that you shoot straight with them and if there's a problem, it has to be talked about honestly and not sugar coated. If it's a hard solution, that's all right, but you have to deal with that in a way where people would say it reflects the trust they have put in you."

Trust is not established quickly. "I don't think you put somebody in the position of running a company and instantly he's trusted," said Gary Nelon. "He has to show every day that he can be trusted. It's a proving period, and like character, you can develop it all your life and lose it in a heartbeat by something you do or something you say."

TRUE LEADERS' PHILOSOPHIES ABOUT TRUST

While most leaders agree that trust ultimately must be earned, different people take different approaches as to how they develop trust from the people who work for them. "My own way is that if I just met you, you have started out with a huge bank account of trust," says Bruce Simpson, CEO of AppGenesys. "I tend to trust everybody until they do something to demonstrate to me that they are not worthy of that trust. Other people I know start with a little more cynical view of the world. They basically believe people are not worthy of trust until they have actually done things to demonstrate that they are trustworthy. Neither thought is good or bad—its just part of the experiences of life I guess. If you get burned too often early on, you might develop a more cynical view than if you have always had good experiences with people." When Simpson took over as the new CEO at AppGenesys, he told his team that because they were new at working together, they had not had the time to develop a two-way trust. "So we all start with some level of trust between each other," he told them, "but we will all be tested mutually. It is through those tests that you develop a real trust."

Simpson relates building trust to the foxhole mentality in the military, where people who depended upon each other for their life developed such a high level of trust that it often endured forever. "In business, you almost have to do the same thing," Simpson says. "It's not the good times that test trust and stretch the limits, it's really when you are put into a difficult situation."

Simpson also points out that the term *trustworthiness* can sometimes be confusing. People do things that are unethical. "Is that trustworthy?" he asks. "Or, when you give me your commitment to do something and you fail to do it, is that untrustworthy? Or is it people that say one thing and do something else that is untrustworthy? If I find somebody that is untrustworthy, it depends on the situation for me.

"On the ethical side—you steal from here—there are no second chances. Period." Simpson says setting very clear boundaries about certain ethical issues and making it clear that they apply to everyone—no exceptions—is important. As an example—when someone is allowed to cheat on an expense account, it can send a mixed message that it's okay to steal a little bit. "That type of rationale is inexcusable," says Simpson. "If you steal you steal, and that's just about all there is to it."

Then there's the issue of trust with people who don't honor their commitments. "I think that's a much bigger and more prevailing area." Simpson cites the example of an employee who says he or she will do a specific thing. "I say, great, I trust you, you're going to go out and do it. And then it doesn't get done. The employee says he got distracted or something else came up. I say, well, if that's the case, why didn't you come back to me and tell me that you couldn't fulfill those commitments because I trusted you to deliver your piece?" Simpson says at this point, depending on the maturity level of the person, this is a coaching opportunity. "But," he cautions, "it goes back to consistency. If this is the first time it's happened and it's a relatively junior person, that's a great opportunity to coach that person. If it's a senior person who should certainly know better, you can always coach them one time. But I will think, wait a minute, you're in a senior position and you don't understand the meaning of trust and commitment? Then I question how you got there in the first place.

This is where you may need to stand back and look at the real issue, according to Simpson. "Typically, we hire people because we think they have value. If we find out very quickly we made a mistake, let's not invest a lot more time. But, if it's somebody that's been with the firm for a while, especially as it has progressed, let's not throw away that investment. We're not talking about ethical, legal types of breaches, but more behavioral issues—let's not throw away that investment. We must have thought pretty highly of the person to promote them in the first place. Right? Let's see if there is a way that we can retain the value and put the person back into roles in which they can play a better position. I have fired very few people in my life. Even the times when people have parted ways with me, I haven't viewed it as a firing, but more of a discussion in which we have come to a conclusion that maybe their own personal business life would be better served someplace else."

The word *commitment* surfaces a lot when talking to true leaders about trust. Dan Woodward says that commitment is the centerpiece of Enherent's value system. "Whether it's a customer or a colleague, helping people to understand what a commitment is and what it is not is important," he says. "'Maybe I'll try' is not a commitment. You can, however, commit to commit, like—I'll let you know by Friday if I can do that by the following Friday. But a commitment doesn't exist unless there's a date and time specified that something is to happen. I try to reinforce that. I think that is what sets the stage and creates opportunities for trust and for relationships to be established."

John Bruck, of BHE Environmental, has a unique way of demonstrating what he means when he talks about establishing his own credibility and trust. "I'm a visual person. The way I try to teach and demonstrate trust is by explaining that you can picture me as an Old West gunslinger that is able to throw plates up and shoot them. When I tell you I'm going to throw a plate up and shoot it, I will. Or if I tell you I'm going to throw three plates up in the air and shoot them, I will—I promise you that. And the best way to develop trust is to do that—just live up to your promises. In return, that's what I expect. I expect people to be able to throw plates up in the air and shoot them when we agree that that's what they are going to do. When they don't, trust begins to erode." Bruck says that when trust erodes, you begin to get hardening of the communication arteries. "People all of a sudden begin to consider themselves isolated and vulnerable." Sometimes people develop an attitude that they are doing their jobs just fine, and how dare anyone think they are not. "That doesn't do anybody any good," Bruck says. "When people begin to build walls, they believe that they are invulnerable. It's important to get them to replace invulnerability with trust." One of the ways Bruck does that is to encourage people to admit mistakes. "If it's a mistake that was a well informed mistake—somebody made a decision and they collected the information they should have and proceeded in a logical way and it resulted in a mistake—they learned from the mistake. I think those kinds of mistakes need to be packaged and promoted as a successes." If, however, the mistake is one that has been made time in and time out, or if it's made without considering information that should have been considered, Bruck believes those mistakes need to be handled more critically. "I think that people who make mistakes, whether for good or for bad, need to own up to them and be accountable for those mistakes. Going back to the leader, I think people trust leaders more if those leaders also talk about the mistakes they make."

At Plante & Moran, a large factor in the company making *Fortune*'s best places to work list was trust in management. "Two-thirds of our score on that *Fortune* list was based on a confidential survey of our staff, and we never got to see the answers. One of the biggest thrusts of the questions they asked was about trust in management of the firm," said Bill Matthews. "Trust in the management of the firm is unbelievably important. If our people did not have trust in the leadership of the firm, I don't think we could have a successful firm. And we work very hard at making sure that we don't tell them things that are not true—no sugar coating—not kidding them—not having them feel like we're not really leveling with them." So how does Plante & Moran create this kind of a trusting environment? By having the people feel like they are trustworthy, according to Matthews. "That's all part of the caring," he explains. "We're not here to have these people generate a lot of revenue for us. Our primary purposes here are to serve our clients and to provide successful careers for our staff. And if they don't believe that we're trying to provide successful careers for them, we don't have a lot going for us."

Matthews admits that one of the challenges is to make sure there is room at the top for those who aspire to the partnership level. "A part of that is why you have to grow the firm," he says. "Our goal is to provide growth. So we provide opportunity for those people, and we've done a reasonably good job at it." Matthews also points out that not everybody is made out to be a partner in a CPA firm. "A lot of people leave and go into industry because they don't like the challenges of public accounting," he says. "A lot of people go make more money in private industry. But I think they also give us credit for having developed them or having gotten them to that point. We treated them well when they were here and helped to develop them and got them to a point where they got a good job somewhere else, and hopefully they are happy where they are and continue to have good relationships with us. Again, I want to reiterate, there are exceptions and we are not perfect. But, as Frank [Frank Moran, the Cofounder who is now deceased] would say, we just want to make sure we have a very good batting average—that's the important thing."

Trust is a core value at Sleep America. President Debbie and CEO Len Gaby say they run their business very tight and very loose and that those two operate simultaneously. While that may sound incongruent, the Gabys say it means that they hold certain values very tight and very dear, around which there is no negotiating, because they are vitally important in establishing the organization's environment of trust. About other issues, they are more flexible and relaxed.

"The first issue that we are very tight on is honesty," says Len Gaby. "We are totally honest with each other and with our customers. Sometimes that is difficult because we don't always like to hear the truth. And sometimes our customers don't like to hear the truth. So we have to be considerate about how we express the truth, but there is no substitute." That includes being truthful about disappointments regarding deliveries, should that happen. "We don't create little white lies to make them feel better. We tell them the truth."

The second tightly held value is mutual respect. "We always have to treat each other with mutual respect. There are a lot of companies where they verbally abuse people, and it becomes productive to the company goals, but short term only. Well, we don't allow that. A salesperson can't call somebody up in the warehouse and beat up on the person [verbally] because they made a mistake. They can all be tolerant of each other's mistakes and cannot abuse each other. They have a responsibility to each other. So honesty becomes a corporate imperative." When honesty and mutual respect prevail, they establish a strong foundation of trust.

TRUST-BUILDING TACTICS

True leaders use various ways to demonstrate and build trust. Following are some examples.

Share

Founder Jack Kahl believes that although business is run for profit, the way you build trust in your culture is to share the wealth. At Manco, information is shared at monthly meetings—the balance sheet, the profit and loss, where the company is at, everything that is going on. "Can you imagine going to a baseball game totally in the dark, where there is no sound, no idea of balls and strikes, and you don't know who's on first or anything—there is no feedback? Do you know what a boring place that would be? Would you want to go to a ball game like that?" Kahl asks rhetorically. "No," he responds. "Yet that's most of the American workplaces. They don't tell you anything. They hide all the information for whatever reason." When Kahl asks fellow leaders why they don't tell their people where the company is and how it's doing, the response he generally gets is, "Well, if they knew how much money we were making, they'd ask for a raise." Kahl's response to that is, "Well, you dummies, why don't you give it to them if they're worth it. Otherwise you're going to lose them to people that are willing to give feedback." So Manco has no big secrets. Information is shared openly and willingly.

At The Container Store, Cofounders Kip Tindell and Garrett Boone also share everything. "*Fortune* told us that 70 percent of the criteria [for being one of the best companies to work for] has to do with what they call the trust index. They said we scored the highest on the trust index. I think all our communications has a lot to do with that," Tindell says. Boone agrees. "The trust in our company comes from all directions. It's not measuring the trust people feel for Kip and myself. We're part of it, but certainly no more so than the people who work in the stores. It's saying I trust the people I work with—I like them. I trust them to be there. I trust them to do a really good job. I trust them to care as much as I care. I trust them to help me and not to stand in the back and use me as a stepping-stone to their career, but that we are in this together and I trust them to support me. Trust is something that has to come from everybody, and it certainly has to be there with the top people in the company."

Part of building that trust is talking to people and letting them know what is going on in the company. Boone says, "We have staff meetings that are anywhere from two to four times a year with everybody from store managers to sales managers from all of the stores, and sometimes [other] people that the store manager wants to send. Everybody in the corporate office is invited. All the distribution managers and supervisors attend. So you have this companywide meeting where everybody talks about everything we are doing—the past, the present, the future—the goals, whether we hit them, what our financial performance is. Then all the information discussed is made up into this magazine, and everybody in the company gets a copy of it—part-time people, seasonal people, anybody who is working for us at the time."

Additionally, every store, every day, gets sales reports that show all 22 stores—not just their store, but every store in the company—every single day. "I think that creates trust," Boone says. "In most retail organizations, even the store manager probably doesn't get information about other stores' sales—maybe the district or something, but not the whole company. Most companies are stingier than heck when it comes to praising people and getting out information," Boone says. Not The Container Store.

Open Communications

Employees at TD Industries also receive all of the company financials. Jack Lowe says another thing they do to create trust is to encourage no structured lines of communication. "We have a pretty broadly held understanding that lines of communication and lines of authority are totally different," Lowe explains. "It is not uncommon for people to bring their concerns to me or to others and they are free to go anywhere they want—anywhere they think they can get help. Everybody knows who their boss is—that's the line of authority. Communications is anybody—you can talk to anybody."

At the GAO, David Walker said that the lack of trust in the organization was evident to him when he took over his role. "One of the first things that I wanted to do was to open up communications. I figured out a way that I could end up helping people to get to know me as a person and to not only open up communications between myself and all of our employees, but to try to encourage other levels of the organization to do the same thing. One example was that I decided I would go to every office that we had in the United States within the first year. I did that within about ten months." In addition, Walker initiated closed circuit videocasts for all employees, which provided an opportunity for people to ask questions. He also encouraged people to communicate with him electronically. "I ended up doing employee feedback surveys with employees, allowing them to be able to send me things in confidence that I would be willing to consider."

Walker also believes that leading by example helps to establish trust. "Practice what you preach," he says. "Don't ask anybody to do something that you wouldn't do yourself. Do your best at whatever you do. If you make a mistake, admit it and try not to make it again. Don't worry about things you can't control—there are so many people that just get all knotted up about things they can't control. Be fair, open, and honest. It's not rocket science," he says, "but it does make sense."

Live Up to Your Commitments

At Feedback Plus, Vicki Henry remembers a time about ten years ago when money was tight—so tight, she didn't take a paycheck for herself. "But I made sure they got theirs," Henry said of the employees. "I didn't tell the people about it [her not paying herself], but they knew." The camaraderie of everyone in the company is a strong reflection of the trust that has been built in the company, Henry says. "One year, we didn't have the best year in the world. At Christmas time, employees were used to getting a little bonus, but we really didn't have much to give. We cut a $100 check for everybody across the board. At the time, we had about 30 employees. One of our young men, Reggie, with two little kids, had been diagnosed with cancer in early December. And I don't know the exact number, but I can tell you that a good many people gave their hundred dollars to Reggie. I think that's wonderful." In an environment of trust, people make an effort to look out for one another as well as the company.

Create Ownership

At PVS Chemicals, Jim Nicholson has set up individual companies within the overall corporate structure. As an example, Nicholson points to one such company that has a group of 54 truck drivers and is set up to have its own set of books and its own president. "Those truck drivers know what their sales are, what their costs are, and what their earnings are for each month. We want them to know because people want to know. And if you don't tell them, they'll guess and they will always guess wrong. They'll see 54 trucks go out of there every day and they'll see the freight rate and they'll multiply, but they'll forget that you have single-business tax and that you have stationery to buy, and so they just do enough [calculating] to give them the wrong answers. If you don't tell them when times are good, then they won't believe you when you tell them times are bad. So you consistently give them the numbers, because they are the ones who can affect the numbers. It all affects their profit sharing and their bonuses. It also helps them to take some ownership because now they know that they are playing a role. If they leave their truck running when diesel fuel is $2 a gallon, the profit sharing will go down.

"It also says something to them about the fact that you think they are adults and they have dignity—that they are old enough and worthy enough to share information with. Now, let me ask, why wouldn't you tell them? You wouldn't tell them because you're afraid of them for some reason. You're afraid they'll use the knowledge to your detriment, or I don't know what. We've done this for 30 years. It hasn't been to our detriment, it has been to our good." Once again, sharing information helps to establish trust.

Model Trust

At Tricon, David Novak says he believes a trusting environment comes when someone believes they are valued and recognized for being able to do the job. "You have to start out with a belief in each other. Trust can't come unless you believe in each other. I can't totally empower you unless I believe you have the capability to do the job. So I think that you have got to make sure that you have leaders who are very set on making sure that they have people who are capable of doing the job, because that's the first start of trust." Next, he says, it's about doing what you say. Repeating one of his favorite quotes, Novak says, "People judge you more by your actions than your intentions. So I think what leaders have to do is first make sure you have someone who has the skills to do the job they are in, and then really value doing what you say you will. When people don't do what they say, you have to take action in terms of coaching. Coach and coach, and then if they don't respond, you have to get them off your team. That creates a trusting environment because people know that if you don't do what you say, you aren't going to be around here. If you tolerate that kind of stuff, then as a leader, you're never going to have a trusting environment."

Ensure Public Trust

"A year ago, people were promising a lot of things they haven't been able to deliver," says AIPC's Tim Webster. "That is why the market is where it is relative to where it was and why our stock just keeps chugging along." Webster says when it comes to market predictions, the key is to have the integrity to say, "We are still building this business for the long haul, and not at the whim of external folks. In fairness to the external folks, they don't know anything about this company other than what we tell them. So if their expectations are out of whack, it is because we guided them off track. So I think you have a tremendous responsibility to communicate realistic expectations." In other words, tell the truth. Webster believes that the pressure to create a long-term growth rate vision for the company that is going to get stock prices up causes a disconnection from what is realistic. "If you get those out of whack, you're going to have to pay the piper sooner or later," he says. "Now, if we can't deliver what we told them, then we have to reshape those expectations. That's what the process is about."

Webster gets pretty intense when he talks about building trust and being realistic and truthful. "A year ago, all you had to do was buy stock. It went up a dollar a day and everyone was getting rich. People were dropping out of all kinds of industries and the idea was a 27-year-old CEO was better than a 55-year-old CEO, because the 55-year-old was hung up with all the ridiculous notions like cost control and policies and procedures and the 27-year-old would let you bring your dog to work. If you weren't a millionaire after 18 months with your company, then get the heck out because you are a dog and you need to get into something else. I think it is just ridiculous and a sign of our society being prone to shortcuts. The honor of a long career and a career of purpose and building something in industry is now boring." Webster also believes we are a pendulum society, and he suspects that its thinking is about to change. For now, he continues to hold tight to his values of telling the truth and trust building.

Whether it is building trust, maintaining trust, or ensuring that a culture of trust endures, true leaders are committed to doing what's right, telling the truth, and continuing to honor the importance of trust.

EXPLORE AND DISCOVER

- What do you do to build trust?

- How realistic are you about your own potential?

- Are you truthful to yourself about your strengths, shortcomings, and potential future?

- How do your employees/colleagues feel about your trustworthiness? How do you know?

- What could you do personally to help enhance trust in your organization?

- How effective are your coaching skills?

- How dependable are you about living up to your commitments?

- How sharing are you with information?

- What fears do you have about disclosure?

- How do you demonstrate openness?

- In what areas of your business or personal life has trust eroded? Why? What are you doing to restore trust?

8

PRINCIPLE SEVEN

Recognize and Build People

True leaders genuinely care about people. They feel a responsibility to create a work environment in which people are respected and recognized, and they allocate funds to ensure that their people are adequately trained. They realize that to sustain profitability and a competitive edge, people make the difference and are their organization's greatest asset. True leaders also recognize that it is their responsibility to set a tone from the top that ensures that their people-building philosophies are adhered to throughout the organization. They encourage people to capitalize on their strengths, they recognize people formally and informally, they provide opportunities, they put systems in place that help to foster continual growth and well-being, and they model an environment of growth through caring, support, and trust.

At PVS Chemicals, Jim Nicholson has a favorite cliché. "The speed of the pack is the speed of the leader," he says. "It works in motorcycle gangs—it works in business." Leaders like Nicholson realize that one of the ways to inspire people is to create high expectations for them by modeling an attitude that earns respect. "First of all, respect is earned, not demanded. You shouldn't be asking people to do jobs you wouldn't do yourself," says Nicholson. Then, he adds, you must provide people with the appropriate tools to do the job. "My rather crude expression is that you can't expect to make chicken salad out of chicken shit. So you've got to give them the right tools to get the job done." Paramount to employees having the right tools is training—training at all levels and various stages. Far too often, training dollars are reserved for the management and senior level people while new hires are provided little more than employee orientation training. Not so at TD Industries and The Container Store.

BUILDING PEOPLE THROUGH A COMMITMENT TO TRAINING

At TD Industries, Jack Lowe has created an environment that sends a very clear message: everyone serves an equally important role in the company's success. For one thing, you won't find Lowe's office in some lofty corner with a typical executive view. He occupies an 8-by-11 foot cubicle right in the middle of the entire office. And he goes beyond an open door policy. "Open door?" Lowe says, with a laugh. "We have a no door policy around here." Only the conference room has a door, and that is only to ensure quietness for meetings and planning sessions. The company also provides "tons of training," says Lowe. "We expect everybody in the business to have a minimum of 32 hours in a classroom each year—all of which we pay for." Training starts the second month after an employee is hired, and the first topic consists of a full day of culture training. About a year later, employees get another day of management training, and a year later they receive two days of quality orientation. If an individual is in any type of a leadership role, they are put on the leadership track for one day of leadership training each year for the next four years. Lowe says more than half the people in the company are on the leadership track—not just supervisors and managers.

Culture training for new hires was not always provided. A few years ago, Lowe shifted his attitude about investing in new hires, deciding that if the company did more for the employees early on, maybe they would understand the culture, embrace it, and stay longer. It worked. "Even new people like working here and are proud to work here," Lowe points out—information that comes from surveys filled out by employees for the *Fortune* recognition. Mentoring is another commitment made to new employees. Mentors are always someone other than the employee's boss, and they are trained and certified. On the construction side of their business, matching a mentor for six months was difficult because of the mobility of field jobs. So, to be sure new people in the field would also be mentored, 100 construction field employees were trained. Together, they devised a system where the new guy on the construction project wears a different colored hat than the seasoned employees. "So, if the new guy shows up on the job and you and I are out there and we are both mentors, we kind of look at each other and decide which one of us is going to mentor the new guy as long as he's on the project," Lowe explains. The adapted system has worked well in the field.

Although Lowe is hard pressed to put a dollar figure on the payback of training, he is adamant that training pays big dividends toward recognizing and building people. "I think if you pull somebody out of their workday and put them in a pretty good training program, you have said something to them about how valuable they are. This ROI [return on investment] on training—I think—is nuts," Lowe says. Some people try to measure the value of training, but Lowe has given up. He just knows it works.

Down the street from TD Industries in Dallas, Texas, is another one of the *Fortune* best companies to work for—The Container Store. Cofounders Garrett Boone and Kip Tindell have a similar philosophy. During an employee's first year of employment at the retailer, they are given 240 hours of formal training in an industry that averages 8. "This is just the formal training," Tindell points out. "Everything from point of sale register training to foundation principle training, to lots and lots of product training." Tindell notes that most retailers don't spend a lot of time training new employees because the industry tends to have a high turnover rate. However, he says their dedication to training has actually lowered their turnover rate by building the people and giving them the tools they need to take care of customers—an integral part of the company's philosophy. Tindell also believes the training insulates the company from its competition very nicely, giving them a distinctive competitive advantage.

BUILD PEOPLE BY BUILDING AN ENVIRONMENT OF CLEAR EXPECTATIONS AND RESPECT

CEO Frank Hennessey expects employees to embrace the culture of MascoTech and to commit to working as a team to help everybody grow and develop toward the best they can be. "I really expect that they will be committed, that they will have high integrity, and that they will respect people," Hennessey says of his employees. He doesn't believe in a controlling environment yet, on the other hand, he does want people to realize that some commitments are non-negotiable—like making certain commitments in terms of goals or objectives. "But we always do it in a way that respects our people," he stresses.

At American Italian Pasta Co., Tim Webster addresses the issue of job security right up front. "Security and safety come from being a part of the team, relying on one another, loving one another, trusting one another, and enjoying seeing each other in the morning when they come in," he says. "But that doesn't mean resting on our laurels and it doesn't mean complacency. I say to them, you know, job security does not come from a union contract or 20 years of service. It comes from being the best. That is the only way you absolutely have job security. It comes from taking care of your customers and making sure your niche is happy customers." Webster says the cornerstone of rewarding people for embracing the culture and strengthening it is constantly giving people more responsibility. "We have widely understood expectations that this is not always going to work," Webster confesses. "But we celebrate that, and virtually every one of us in the top leadership positions have gone through some aspect of role expansion or role contraction, because human development and growth is not linear. The notion that your company is going to grow at exactly the same pace of all your people is absolutely ludicrous," Webster says. "People are influenced by their external life, whether it is their financial scenario, their marriage, their church, or their kids. They are going to go through changes and calculations that affect their ability to concentrate and commit to the purpose of the company. So we constantly promote people and put them into more and more responsibility. If you do a good job, we reward it with more responsibility and more money—that's how it works." Webster admits that on the occasions that it doesn't work, those can be okay, too. He points to a time when he promoted someone before he was ready. "This young man did such a good job that he immediately got two more jobs layered on top, and we saw him disappearing into the quicksand under the weight of all that. It was very disappointing to him, but we picked him up, took him all the way back to the position he started in, rebuilt his confidence, got his sea legs back under him, and now he is an executive vice president with a wide array of responsibilities. So human development is not linear; it is a series of plateaus. We celebrate that aspect of human dynamics."

While some executives may suggest that building an environment that recognizes and builds people is easier in the private sector than in the public sector, most true leaders would disagree. Gary McDaniel, CEO of the publicly held Chateau Communities, says, "I think a leader has a responsibility to provide a positive work environment, to provide a salary and compensation package that is competitive, and to provide the kind of a place where people like the folks that they are working with and feel good about going to work everyday. A lot of times, particularly in the public company environment, folks talk about creating shareholder value and doing a good job for the board of directors. To me, that's ludicrous. That stuff all comes, but you have to provide the environment for the people in the company first—they are the most important."

David Novak agrees. As Chairman and CEO of Tricon Global Restaurants, Novak sees his leadership role as a tremendous opportunity to create an environment for happier jobs. He says his attitude goes back to his childhood. Novak was raised by a mom and dad who taught him the importance of having respect for people. He also acknowledges that he grew up in a very humble background, yet because of parents who provided opportunities for him that they personally never had, he was able to accomplish much. "I would rather go through life impacting and creating a better environment for 600,000 employees [the number of employees he is responsible for worldwide] or team members than go through life just going through the motions. My dad and my mom worked their tails off, and I see my mom and dad in our business every day. I think that my mom and dad could have been company presidents, but somehow they didn't get the opportunity. I have. So how am I going to treat people like my mom and dad? I'm going to treat them well."

Novak makes it clear, however, that treating people well doesn't mean that you can't make tough decisions or expect high performance. "I think if you talk to people that work with me, they wouldn't question my standards. But, deep down, I believe that people and teams make it happen. You show me anything that's been done that hasn't been done by people working together. People who don't understand that are the people who think they can do it all by themselves. Those people are not very successful." Even if Novak were just out for sheer results, he says he would still come down to the rationale that it is important to create happy environments and to recognize people, simply because people drive the business. Recognizing people is simply the winning formula for success, according to Novak. "I'm very competitive. I like to win and I hate losing. We just had a bad year and I did not like that—it was the first year of my entire business career where we didn't make my personal business plan. That was very hard for me to take, but that doesn't mean my formula for success is going to change."

BUILD PEOPLE BY RECOGNIZING THEM

Novak also believes that one of the ways you recognize people is by allowing them a self-discovery process. "The best idea anyone ever had is one they came up with themselves," he says. "So I think great companies really work on self-discovery." He also believes in coaching. "I've come to find out that there are two reasons people leave our company—or any company. It's not because of money. It's because they don't get along with their boss and they don't feel valued." That's why Novak has changed all supervisory titles to coach and has made recognition an integral part of leadership development. "We have awards all around the world," Novak says. At Pizza Hut, they give a Big Cheese Award. The President of Taco Bell gives The Order of the Pepper Award. In Australia, they give the Flying Pig Award, and the CEO for International gives a Golden Glove Award. There is also a Yum Award—a set of talking teeth, which is given for putting the "yum" on the customer's face around the world. Before heading up Tricon, when Novak was president of Kentucky Fried Chicken, he spontaneously gave away the Rubber Chicken Award. "I'd go find a cook in the house who had worked for 30 years, and I'd go to my briefcase and get out a floppy chicken. I'd write something on it like, 'Here's to Bill, thanks for making great original recipe for 30 years—you're what makes this company really tick—thank you very much.' I'd bring the whole team together and give him a $100 gift certificate because you couldn't eat the floppy chicken." Why a floppy chicken instead of a plaque? "Because everybody gives away plaques and we wanted to have fun. Our business is fun, so everything we do needs to drive home what the business is all about." Even today, Novak continues to give silly awards. And when he does, he takes photos and sends one to the person given the award and hangs the other in his office. "If you saw my office, it is like floor to ceiling pictures of people," says Novak. "It's the greatest office in America."

At the senior leadership level, Novak teaches a leadership course that he developed himself. An integral part of the course is having everyone fill out a personal contract—a contract with the people. Asked what his own contract says, Novak willingly pulls a sheet of paper out of his wallet and reads from it: *"Stay focused on what really matters—people and customers—the stock will take care of itself. Consistently include and articulate our strategies and culture and stay in the upper mood state by starting each day by recognizing how grateful I am for the blessings I receive."* Novak is incredibly proud of his contract, and it helps him to practice what he preaches as he travels around the world.

Garrett Boone believes that leaders lead by both words and examples. "I think it's hard to do it just by words alone," says the cofounder of The Container Store. People want to see action. So Boone visits his retail stores frequently, and when he does, he is very conscious of the company's foundation principles and makes sure that he models them. "When I visit a store, there are certain times I work on the floor. The time that I'm on the sales floor, I want to make sure that I'm doing exactly what we are preaching. It shows everybody that I think that is a really important thing to do, that it's worth my time doing, and also that I hold myself to the same standards to live up to. Our job is not to just wander around until somebody comes up and taps us on the shoulder and says, 'Can you help me, please?' Our job is to engage the customer in conversation." Boone makes sure that his words and actions are one in the same. He also believes it's important for him to interact personally with individual employees when he visits stores and to recognize them for the job they are doing. "Most people don't expect people with titles to even recognize them. That's pretty astounding. So it's pretty easy to go counter to that if that's what you really believe and want to do, because in a retail store setting, if you take time to visit with everybody in the store, that's encouraging to people. That's like saying, I must be relatively important."

When Boone works in the store, there is little he won't do. He helps customers by doing carry outs, he picks up trash off the floor, and he waits on people who have no idea that he is one of the founders. "I think that's another way of my saying to our people that I really respect what they do," says Boone. "It's talking to people, recognizing them, asking them their ideas. Even when I call a store, I'll spend time talking to the person that answers the phone. I'll say, 'This is Garrett,' and I'll just go on and talk to them as if they were the primary person I called. I learn a lot of information from them. That's part of the trust, really. Trust is something that has to come from everybody, and it certainly has to be there with the top people in the company because if you don't have it there—you don't have it."

At Weight Watchers International, Linda Huett recognizes the diversity of her people's talents by taking them out of silos. "Whenever I see a silo mentality—in other words, this is *my* corridor and I don't expect input or interference from the outside—what I try to do is say that we are not individual corridors or these closed little tunnels, which are only our part of the business. All of us have an effect on everything else that is happening, because usually what one corridor is doing actually does have a big effect on some other part of the business. So making sure that everybody can have a say and be listened to, even if it is outside of their discipline, is important." Huett cites the marketing area as an example, saying that all too often people in marketing believe that only marketers should have an opinion about what is going on with the marketing strategy. "But the truth is, the whole organization is impacted by our marketing, and many senior managers without a marketing background have very valuable contributions to make our marketing plans better and more effective." If the leader doesn't establish any forums for shared thinking to happen, then people become isolated in their thinking and valued in only specific areas. Huett's approach provides the dual benefit of maximizing input, while recognizing that everyone's thinking is important and valued.

BUILD PEOPLE BY DOING SOMETHING SPECIAL

While organizations often have a corporatewide philosophy that everyone must be treated equally, in reality, sometimes exceptions are appropriate. Gary Nelon believes being there for your people when they have unexpected problems is important. "Whenever somebody's got a problem, you go and take care of it," says the Chairman of First Texas Bancorp. "Whether it's a personal problem or a business-related problem, you make sure that they know that you care in a deep and passionate way. To me, it's in the little things." Nelon knows firsthand the importance of little things because of what his boss once did for him early in his banking career. Nelon and his wife were taking a trip to Hawaii. On a Sunday afternoon before the trip, Nelon had an unexpected appendectomy attack and ended up having surgery that night at midnight. "At seven o'clock the next morning, I woke up, and the person standing beside my bed was Leon Stone [Nelon's boss]. 'Well, I guess you're not going to be able to make the trip to Hawaii next Sunday,' Stone said. About that time the surgeon walked in, and I said, 'Doctor, what is the recovery treatment for this kind of surgery?' 'Walking,' the doctor replied. 'Lots of walking.' I looked up at the doctor and said, 'Well, can't I walk just as well in Hawaii as I can walk here?'" Nelon's boss agreed and promised the doctor that he'd make sure that the bags were packed and that Nelon wouldn't have to lift them, and the doctor agreed that Nelon could go on the trip. "It's that kind of thing," Nelon said. "It's just being there when something is not going just right."

Mike McCarthy made a decision to treat one of his building company employees differently because he thought it was the right thing to do under the circumstances. The husband of an employee got cancer. The employee was not able to do her job very well and struggled with some severe emotional problems. For a time she went on disability. When disability ran out, she needed to go back to work because she needed the money for the medical problems. McCarthy found a job for her that required much less pressure than her previous job, and allowed her to return on a part-time basis and move gradually back to a full-time basis. "Now, could we find someone better to do that job?" McCarthy asked. "Yes," he admitted. "And is she free of her emotional problems? No," he confessed. "Does she do the job well? Yes, and we've taken care of her." McCarthy thinks it's important to take care of people when you can. He's even established a rather unusual program to take care of people's unexpected problems. "We have something called the McCarthy Emergency Family Relief Fund," he explained. "It's instant dollars for either McCarthy employees or just someone the employees know who is having problems. Let's assume that your house just burned down and you have kids and you have nowhere to sleep. If we hear about it, we give you dollars right now. All you have to do is clear with one person. Your advocate comes in and talks to one person in the company, and we will give you enough dollars to get you to a point where you can get help from a community agency if you need extended help." McCarthy says that most leaders he respects spend a good part of their time giving back to either their community or to disadvantaged people. McCarthy encourages his employees to become involved in the community and its charitable activities. "One of the reasons I get our people involved in charitable organizations is to get a larger view of who they are. To the extent that you are giving to other people, you feel better about yourself," he says. "I don't think money alone makes it in any organization. If your organization is solely devoted to money, I don't think you have values that are going to attract and keep the kind of people that are going to stay with you." The average McCarthy employee has been with the company between 17 and 19 years, McCarthy notes proudly. "When you look at the entire attractiveness of an employee to our company, it's participation, it's being trained, it's having someone have affection for not only your needs but your family's needs. If you have a problem with your family, you're not abandoned—we will try to help you. It's a participation in the company's profits, in the company's stock, and lots of parties, celebrations, and pats on the back. It's a lot of instantaneous kinds of things to recognize the fact that you did something really neat here at McCarthy."

McCarthy's Southwest Division President, Bo Calbert, relates the impact from an employee's viewpoint. "There's something about McCarthy that's got to be very unique in that I've never felt that I wasn't a part of a bigger picture—that it was more than just a job," says Calbert. "For the 19 years I've been with McCarthy, I never ever worried about the next job, and in construction, it's a industry that is notorious for hiring people for a project and then laying them off and hiring them again the next project. I never, ever worried about when that next opportunity was going to come and what it was going to be." Calbert says that as a member of the senior leadership team, he conveys that sense of belonging to people when he interviews potential hires. "When I interview them, I tell them we're not hiring you for the job, we're hiring you for the career. I think that's pretty unusual for the construction industry." And once an engineer is hired, they get immersed with the McCarthy spirit early. "Every year, we have a new hire orientation program where all the new recruits—the new engineers that were hired for that year—go to St. Louis for a week of orientation," Calbert explains. "I can remember that first trip to St. Louis when I was a young engineer. Mike [McCarthy] told us he wanted to be the best builder in America, and nobody really knew what that meant and nobody really felt that we would know when we got there. But it was kind of a passion that I had, and that everybody else had, to work toward. And it means a lot more than being the richest builder. I'm not sure that even today I know exactly what that means, but it's a lot more than bottom-line profits. I think anyone who has a passion to do something really great wants to have a goal that is much greater than just being dollar driven. I want to walk away with a lot of pride and accomplishment, and being the best builder in America means a lot more than just making money. It means you take care of your clients, you take care of your people, and you build some wonderful projects. And the reason our people love being in the building business anyway is because the things that you build and walk away from you get to walk back to 10, even 20, years from now and take your kids and your grandkids and show them what you've done. A bank account can never represent that in the same way."

Brent Hardman, who worked for Managing Director Ann Hambly in various companies before following her to Prudential Asset Resources, demonstrates a similar perspective by sharing an example of Hambly's sensitivity during a personal crisis he encountered a few years ago. Hardman's father had been hospitalized miles away, and his situation worsened. When people at the hospital tried to reach Hardman, they could not, so they got hold of his boss. Hambly, in turn, had to let Hardman know that his father was dying. "It was a horrible thing to have to do, and she was so kind," Hardman recalled. "I was so upset that she made sure someone drove me to my apartment. I got on the phone, trying to get airfare to Los Angeles, and it was thousands of dollars and I didn't have the cash right then. She said she had frequent flyer miles saved and got on the phone and made all the arrangements within an hour." Hardman points out that, while this is a personal example of how Hambly really cares about her people, it isn't isolated to him. "It's not just me. She would do that for any loyal employee. There is nothing she wouldn't do for you. I feel very lucky. Not many people have that type of environment—it's very rare."

BUILD PEOPLE BY LEARNING FROM MISTAKES AND CREATING OPPORTUNITIES

Mistakes happen. Most are unintentional and need to be recognized as such say most of the leaders interviewed. The important thing about mistakes is to own up to them, deal with them, and learn from them. David Walker, the Comptroller General of the United States, says, "You've got to make mistakes—no risk, no return, no innovation. The key is to learn from them and try not to repeat them—try not to make dumb mistakes." At Weight Watchers, Linda Huett encourages people to talk about things that didn't work. "There is a tremendous amount of fear about blame," she says. "So if you can get rid of the blame and just take responsibility—and responsibility just means this is what I did, this why I did it, this is how I did it, and in retrospect, we could have done this." At Tricon, David Novak uses a basketball analogy to demonstrate why it is important to treat mistakes as learning points and give people a second chance. "If you are throwing a pass to somebody, you want to know that they can catch it," Novak says. "So if I throw a pass to you and you have scored before, I know you just made a mistake this time, so I'm going to throw it to you again. A shooter has got to keep shooting. If you know the person can make the shot, a great coach doesn't say don't shoot anymore after they miss two shots in a row. A great coach says, 'Keep shooting—it's going to fall.' A leader has to say, 'Keep shooting.'" Novak also says the leader's responsibility is to model how to deal with mistakes by being accountable for their own. "Recognize that you are not going to be right all the time. That's why it's so important to have really talented people that you believe in. You just have to get up off the floor and get out there again." It all begins with the leader's own accountability, which sets the tone.

Create Opportunities

It's very easy to get into a trap of focusing on mistakes instead of looking for positive opportunities. If leaders can shift the emphasis to looking for the things people are doing that are right and for ways to reward doing the right thing by creating opportunities, they serve the organization better and go a long way toward building people. "I think my definition of leadership has changed over the years," says Len Gaby, CEO of Sleep America. "I really see it today as being in a position to help people become all that they can be—to really give them the opportunity to achieve whatever their goals are and be successful in their own right. There is no greater reward for me than to see somebody who we hired in a capacity of sweeping the floor in the warehouse become in charge of all the receiving processes in our warehouse." Gaby was speaking about an actual situation that happened in one of their Phoenix stores. "We have a young man who barely speaks English, yet we were able to recognize that he had an incredible mind. He's literally brilliant. We have 30,000 square feet of warehouse with over 3,000 pieces of merchandise, and he could tell you exactly where every piece is. So we were able to recognize his skill and ability and put him in a position where he now directs everything that happens in that warehouse. He started at $7 an hour, and today I perish the thought of living without him." Gaby reiterates, "That's what leaders do—help people achieve their own personal success."

At the public accounting firm of Plante & Moran, Bill Matthews also believes a leader has the added responsibility of recognizing possible successors. "When you become office managing partner or Managing Partner of the firm, the first job you have is to start figuring out your successor," Matthews says. "And, as Chairman, how will I find out who that successor is, and how will I develop that person to be my successor? It is very important for the future of the firm that each of us develops a successor, delegates, and helps people become everything they can become." Matthews says that currently at least three or four people could be the firm's next Managing Partner, but that person is not selected at the outset. Instead, the firm tries to pick a few people and give them the opportunity develop themselves into professional managers. "So for anybody who is in a leadership position in the firm, we feel a big responsibility for them to be able to develop other people to become whatever they can become— to follow up and follow through." That requires taking a sincere interest in the people, giving them the freedom to make choices, to encourage and guide them, and "just have a caring attitude toward their careers without worrying that they are going to take over my job or show me up. Not worrying about yourself and letting them become whatever they can become." Matthews says that his mentor, Frank Moran, used to tell him, "I would like to have this whole firm full of people smarter than I am. That should be your goal—to have a whole firm smarter than you are, because then you'll be in pretty good shape." Matthews says that their firm invests a lot of money in their staff. "We justify it this way— that a happy workforce, a motivated workforce, a motivated staff, will be a more productive staff. Just look at the turnover. Our turnover is half of what the profession's is, so it's a tremendous economic advantage for us. And the fact is, we believe it comes back to the productivity you get from happy people and reduced turnover. Our goal is not to maximize our profitability, our goal is to optimize it." When leaders encourage the whole team to win, everyone wins.

At BHE Environmental, John Bruck realized that shifting everyone's thinking about sick time could be a people-building effort that would be rewarding for the people as well as the company. "Most people in the company considered sick time to be an entitlement—that you got five days of sick time that you could cash in on one way or another throughout the year." So Bruck's leadership team decided that paying sick time was not financially healthy because it didn't contribute to the company's overall success. "Being sick doesn't help a client reach a solution any better or faster," Bruck said. "But being well does. So instead of paying people for being sick, we decided to pay people for being well. Now, if you have appendicitis and have to go to the hospital, obviously there is a place on your time record to show that, and you get paid for it with the company's blessings. We'll probably even send you flowers. But, if you're not sick, we will pay you a day every six months for being well." With the new concept, the company saw a complete elimination of sick time. Since implementing the new concept, employees have had one heart attack, one appendicitis, and one instance where a man fell out of a tree stand and broke both legs while he was deer hunting—all legitimate sick times. People who go to the hospital get support without a problem. But a whole shift has occurred in the way everyone now thinks about sick time—one that benefits both employees and the company.

Following are some additional ways in which interviewees recognize and build their people.

Call Jim Day

PVS Chemical's James Nicholson picks one day a quarter and designates it as Call Jim Day. "You can call up, you don't have to identify yourself, it's just an open direct access for folks to call up and vent or praise or complain," Nicholson explains. It's open to employees, their spouses, even their kids—anyone who wants to call. And there are no filters—no secretary who screens the call and says that Nicholson is not available.

Fun Committee

The Container Store borrowed the idea of a Fun Committee from Southwest Airlines. The committee gets together and decides to do things that are just for fun. Among the past year's events were a chili cook-off and a Wizard of Oz costume party where even the cofounders dressed in costume. On the day we arrived at the corporate office for our interviews, a team of employees in coordinated T-shirts had just finished forming a human arch to send off a group of visiting school kids. They cheered and reestablished the arch for us and greeted us with the same enthusiasm.

Wow Stories

At MascoTech, they created a process for catching people doing something right. They call it *Wow stories.* "Wow story is very simple," explains CEO Frank Hennessey. "It's when you see somebody that's doing something that's absolutely incredible, and you can't help but say, 'Wow!' So we wanted to acknowledge and recognize and reward our people who are living into our vision and who are doing those extraordinary things and making a difference. So we publish stories about them in an internal newsletter." It gives stature to the person that gets coverage, and it also opens up communications as employees call one another to acknowledge what they have read about one another. "People like to be acknowledged for what they do," says Hennessey. "They need to know that you know what they are doing—the contributions that they are making, the sacrifices that they are making, and the successes that they are achieving. People appreciate being recognized."

Handwritten Notes

At American Italian Pasta Co., they have an accolade system. "Every week in my staff meeting, we write accolades for good deeds, good performance, and exceeding expectations," says CEO Tim Webster. "The person that writes it signs it, and then we all sign it. If I'm acknowledging my assistant for helping me with the annual meeting, it is signed by the whole executive staff," Webster says.

Individual Freedom

At Plante & Moran, flextime is nothing new. "As far back as I know, you could start any time you want and go home any time you want," said Managing Partner, Bill Matthews. It is expected that people will be available during normal working hours for their clients and to get their job done. "But whether you come in at 8:00 or 8:30 or 9:00 or 9:30, that's up to you. Your job is to take care of your clients and take care of your staff. We give you a choice—you'll see that in our principles—individual freedom."

While different companies use different strategies to build and recognize people, what is consistent is that true leaders understand the importance of building and recognizing their people and they make sure that either formally or informally, it gets done.

EXPLORE AND DISCOVER

- Are your people provided with all the tools they need to do their jobs effectively?

- Is training provided at all levels within your company?

- Is training adequately helping to build leadership skills, or is it focused on technical hard skills?

- How strong is your company's culture training?

- What is done to ensure that senior leadership's philosophies are understood at all levels of the company?

- What do you do to recognize the good things that people are doing?

- What kind of awards and recognition incentives are given to people in your department?

- What percentage of your time is focused on problems versus what works well?

- How good are you at practicing what you preach?

- What do you do to encourage interdepartmental meetings to foster new thinking?

- What do you do to model an environment that is rich with recognition?

- How do you create opportunities to capitalize on people's strengths?

- What do you do to encourage people to "keep shooting"?

- How do you demonstrate sensitivity to special needs?

- What unique program or concept have you created to foster recognition?

9

Trust Your Intuition

Little has been written about intuition as it pertains to business. In years past, the subject of intuition would likely have been attributed more to personal life than professional life—often tied more to women's thinking than men's. It would have been very common to hear a mother, for example, discuss how she instinctively knew something about her children, and less common to hear a man acknowledge that he had made a business decision based on intuition. Today, the powerful role that intuition plays in the world of business is more accepted. Every leader whom we interviewed acknowledged some acceptance of intuition, and one company even lists intuition as one of its guiding principles.

In today's fast-paced world, organizations need to be agile. They must frequently respond quickly, with a strong sense of urgency. Despite the plethora of easily accessible information, managers also have a sense of overload. Overanalysis can lead to indecisiveness and stalled decision making. In a world where speed is often the greatest differentiating factor, leaders have learned to value that inner sense of knowing called intuition.

The dictionary defines *intuition* as an ability to know something without the conscious use of reasoning. Some call it gut instinct. Some call it judgment. Some call it wisdom. Some refer to it as an inner knowing. Others simply call it what it is—intuition. All agree, however, that intuition should not be confused with guessing or shooting from the hip. Rather, it is a combination of learning and experience that enables one to trust that inner voice that sometimes says no when all the facts say yes.

Fourth on The Container Store's list of six foundation principles is: *Intuition does not come to an unprepared mind. You need to train it before it happens.* The principle further states: *Albert Einstein credited his theory of relativity to a flash of intuition. He was riding on a train and as he watched another train pull past, he felt as if he were moving backwards, an experience most of us have had. However, unlike the rest of us, he suddenly conceived the theory of relativity. Einstein never could have had this insight if he hadn't spent his whole life studying physics and mathematics. The key is for all employees to have an obsession with learning, to then tune in to their intuition and to apply it to almost any business situation.*

Company Cofounder Kip Tindell says "We have always worked to make people realize that intuition does have a role in business. Somebody once said that intuition is merely the sum total of your life experience. It is more than just logic—there is logic and there is intuition." Tindell gives the analogy of fly-fishing, a sport dear to his heart. "I think I'm pretty good at it," he says, "and if I intuitively think a trout is under a rock and I cast over to it, there probably is a trout under the rock. But if you have never fly fished before and you intuitively think there is a trout under the rock, there probably isn't." Tindell says that at The Container Store, they encourage employees to use their intuition. "When you spend more money on training than any retailer in America, you really want people to leverage that training by trusting their intuition. If you teach them all this stuff and they are afraid to extrapolate on that knowledge by trusting their intuition, then you're not getting a full deal on all their training and knowledge."

Garrett Boone, the other cofounder, admits that the company was actually started with a leap of intuition. "We didn't go out and see this concept anywhere. One day the light bulb went off—hey, what about a store that has nothing but things that help people organize their life? The preparation was two years of researching a handmade furniture store and researching commercial products that were kind of neat sounding that had not been retailed before. It turns out that most of those products were things that you store things in, like plastic bins and wire barrels—things like that. So it was the research into something to go with handmade furniture that in the end led to the light bulb going off." When Boone talks to school children visiting the company, he tells them, "Twenty-three years ago, Kip and I started this business with very little money and with an idea—everything you see has come from that idea."

Intuition cannot be taught. Everyone probably has it—some merely fail to recognize it. Ann Hambly with Prudential Asset Resources believes that intuition begins with an ability to have an awareness naturally of what is going on around you. "There are those people in the world who will walk down the middle of the grocery store aisle with their cart in the middle of the aisle," she says, noting that they seem to have no awareness that other people are trying to move down that same aisle. "I don't know if it all falls in this category, but I think being aware of the signals around you and following those things that present themselves is what intuition is about. I think it is very important." Hambly thinks intuition is a combination of awareness, common sense, and your own gut feeling. "I do rely on my gut feeling a lot," she admits. "When I interview people, I can almost always tell within about the first two minutes whether or not I think they are a good fit for the group or not. That is a gut feel—intuition." Hambly also admits that at times she has gone against her intuition—relied on other things and talked herself out of the gut feelings—and realized later that she made the wrong decision. "One wasn't easily correctable," she laments. "I was stuck with it for a long time."

Gary McDaniel bases many of his decisions on how he feels intuitively about things. The CEO of Chateau Industries believes the final decision is probably a combination of experience, practical information, and gut feeling. "The experience and the amount of time allow me to look at things differently than I would have 20 years ago," he says. "But I've always been an intuitive type of person, particularly in dealing with people—making hiring and firing decisions, and the folks that I think can do a good job. I've always been more intuitive on those types of things than on tests or seeing how the person fits into a particular box. I've been burned in the past because of that, but I've also made a lot of good choices because of that." McDaniel, like many executives, can't put a finger on the specifics of intuition. "I'm not quite sure why it happens—it just does."

Even at Plante & Moran, where facts and practicality play an integral role in the field of public accounting, Bill Matthews says intuition is important. He remembers being complimented by his mentor and company Cofounder, Frank Moran, for having intuition. "Frank never told me how smart I was, but he always told me how intuitive I was," Matthews recalled. "So the indication was that I was able to come up with an intuitiveness about the right thing to do or the right answer. And he [Frank Moran] was amazed about that, and pretty soon he had me believing that I was pretty good at that. So I don't know what it is, but I've always felt like I've had a good business sense, common sense, that type of thing. Nobody ever told me I was the smartest person that ever walked the face of the earth, so I've relied on intuitiveness maybe more than I should have over the years. But I would support it by the fact that people thought I had very good judgment and could make good decisions without spending a lot of time on details." Matthews does caution that this doesn't mean one should go off half-cocked because of good intuition. He admits that he has made a few mistakes—"Nothing fatal though," he assures.

Jim Copeland, CEO of Deloitte & Touche, another public accounting firm, warns against getting too caught up in intuitive brilliance. "If you get too caught up in it, it's not a long step to arrogance, and arrogance is the downfall of organizations and individuals." Copeland suggests that flashes of intuitiveness be followed up with some good, hard research and fact-based information. Yet he agrees that sometimes there is no analytical answer. "There are some decisions that really are gut-level of what you think. You can take all the input that you want, but at the end of the day, you've got to call the shot." Copeland isn't quite sure whether that is intuition or if it is simply making the best decision based on all of the best information available. Yet even a hard-core engineer confesses to giving credence to intuition. When determining a viable project for his building companies, Mike McCarthy has learned to trust his gut feelings. "I'm a graduate engineer, so I'll do the plusses and minuses before I make a major decision. But I may total the thing up and it will say 90 percent that I should do it and 10 percent says don't do it, and I won't do it because it just does not feel right. It's really been good that I've trusted my intuition," McCarthy said.

As CEO of PVS Chemicals, James Nicholson regularly uses his economics background to evaluate acquisitions or divestitures, so he pays close attention to the net present value of the future earnings stream. Often, he must make decisions without precise information, so he taps into his previous knowledge and also listens to what his gut is telling him. Over the years, Nicholson says he has seen that reams of data can appear precise, so acting upon the available data is seductive. He has also learned that where his gut said "no" despite the data, his instinct was generally the right decision to follow.

Even in banking, intuition becomes a factor. First Texas Bancorp Chairman Gary Nelon says if you're well enough informed about lots of issues, then all of a sudden within the framework of that knowledge, you have a gut feel as to what needs to be done. You trust the intuitive reactions to determine the steps that need to be taken. "Some people call it following their hearts, some people call it their gut instinct, and some say it just occurs to me. It's based on a whole body of knowledge, how lots of things come together. If you are in a position of needing to make some decisions and you gain all of the feedback you can, you still have to make a decision. At some point between input and decision, there is still that moment when the thought jumps in there that says, 'I think this is what I'll do.' It just occurs to you."

Scientists say that the mind continuously processes information that you are not consciously aware of. They also point out that the brain is intricately linked to other parts of the body via the nervous system and chemical signals. As a result, neuroscientists believe that the mind is actually a combined, intricate system of brain and body, which may explain why intuitive feelings are often linked to physical feelings—a sensation of body chills or a queasy feeling in one's stomach—often referred to as a gut feeling. If, in fact, the intuitive process is natural and useful, then when combined with practicality and facts, it can be very helpful in situations where quick decisions are imperative. It quickens your decision process. "Speed is very important in business," says Tricon's David Novak. "You can get paralyzed by overanalyzing things. I think intuition allows you to see a train wreck coming—it allows you to push people in the right areas. You might not have all the facts, but you are right more than you're wrong. I think the best leaders have an intuition that makes them right more than they're wrong, so it allows you to mine the field right.

"You bring all your experience, your knowledge, the mistakes you've made—all those things come into play. You don't throw those things out. Really being on top of what you've learned in the past and what you've seen other people do—self-awareness and external awareness. That's what really leads to intuition."

The higher up the leadership ladder one climbs, the more important to fine-tune business instincts. In an ever changing, rapidly paced world, intuition may well become the differentiating factor for competing successfully.

EXPLORE AND DISCOVER

- Are you intuitive?

- What words do you use to describe intuition?

- How comfortable are you with trusting your intuition?

- Have you ever experienced a gut feeling that you have ignored and it later proved to be right?

- Do you operate with tunnel vision, or do you have a keen awareness of all that is going on around you?

- Does practicality get in the way of your natural intuition?

- What could you do to increase your intuitive awareness?

- When you reflect on past decisions, what might you learn from them about the power of intuition?

10

Risk to Respond and Grow

In a business world where change has become the status quo, leaders must be willing to take risks to meet the challenges of change. Never before has rapid change so dramatically impacted the results of business decisions. With ever advancing technologies, the scope of knowledge has grown so rapidly that new information takes little time to reach critical mass. So the challenge of leadership becomes an issue of how to assimilate change to enable the organization to grasp opportunities brought forth by change quickly, and at the same time understand that because people absorb change at differing speeds, they will begin to display inefficiency and burnout if they are pushed to behave beyond their maximum thresholds of resiliency. The ultimate leader's challenge is to balance the risk of absorbing major changes with the capacity at which the organization's people can function without suffering burnout and dysfunction.

CULTIVATE AN ENVIRONMENT OF RISK TAKING

The Comptroller General of the United States says that to help the organization understand the need to respond to and move through change, a leader first needs to demonstrate that you are on a burning platform. "By that I mean that the status quo is unacceptable," says David Walker. "That there is a need to change and if we don't change, there are going to be adverse consequences for the institution and/or the individuals. If you want to make as much of a difference as you can make, then we need to make these changes in order to do that." Bill Matthews, of Plante & Moran, says that one of the best ways to foster new ideas for growth is to celebrate people who are able to challenge the status quo successfully. People who are willing to take risks and foster change are demonstrating behaviors that are valued and rewarded.

When people are willing to take risks and challenge the status quo, "You celebrate it, acknowledge it, and champion it," says Matthews. When risks are celebrated, a spirit is created where people feel like taking risks is a good thing to do. "As you know," he says, "change is always difficult and most people don't like change. So you have to try to create an atmosphere where people can think change is looked upon very favorably." Matthews is right. Often individuals resist change because they have a negative perception of how the change will impact them personally. People will view change negatively if they think the challenges created by the change are greater than their capabilities. They will tend to view change more positively if they view their capabilities to be greater than the challenges brought about by the change. In all cases, it is incumbent upon the leader to communicate the impact the changes will have on people personally, because until they see a personal connection between their own behavior and capabilities and the benefit to the organization, the changes will not be personally relevant. A typical example of connecting changes to individuals happens during times of acquisitions, expansions, or mergers.

Matthews points to the growth within their firm as a demonstration of taking risks to grow. At one time, the firm consisted of one office, albeit one of the largest one-office firms in the country. "The feeling was, if we're in other offices, we won't be the same—we won't have the same culture," said Matthews. But they took the risk. Matthews points out that the firm's next managing partner actually opened the Ann Arbor [Michigan] office—their third office at the time. "It's been one of the most successful offices we have today," Matthews said. "Here's a person that is going to be our next managing partner, so you can tell that the firm was very supportive of what he accomplished, along with the team he had. So to go to multiple offices, and even expanding into Ohio, were big challenges for us." Yet the changes resulted in success, the firm now has 15 offices, and they haven't lost the culture.

Another risk Matthews has taken involves sharing information with industry peers. "I'll bet I've given 20 speeches over my career on staff retention and staff development. I take this stuff to them and I talk to them, but the problem is, they think it's an easy fix—a mechanical thing—like how to develop my culture in five easy steps and then I'll be done. But it doesn't work that way. It's built from the beginning, constantly nurtured, and it never ends." Part of the challenge of growth for success is being willing to take the time to implement what has worked well for others—not just gather the information and give lip service to it.

Some leaders have learned to initiate change before it is called for. David Novak says he's never satisfied. "You've always got unfinished business," says the CEO of Tricon. "You always know that we have to do better next year than we did this year, so you play like you're behind even when you're ahead. It basically starts out with the notion that you can always do more than what you've done. You just believe that." The other challenge is not sitting back and defending how far you have come. "You get paid for growth," Novak says. "I see a lot of leaders, who aren't that good as leaders, defend how far they've come. They start to rationalize how much success they've had. You get paid not for what you've done, but for what you are going to do and what you are going to do to make sure that you continue to grow." That doesn't mean you can't recover from a bad year, Novak points out. "It's the mindset that's the key." Novak says if a leader fails to challenge the status quo, the company can become lethargic and underachieving. "I think if a leader can't get you pumped up about what the potential of the company is and doesn't really believe in the business and doesn't have a vision of where you can go, you ought to get another leader."

Ann Hambly says an important part of the process of dealing with change is the seemingly simple act of making a decision. "When I've worked for bosses who don't make decisions, you try to compromise," says the Managing Director of Prudential Asset Resources. "If you have all these great ideas of what to do and you bring them to someone and they sit on them, you generally will compromise your view a lot and will just settle for mundane changes," she says. A decision—good or bad—is better than sitting on things Hambly believes. "I stop and think—what is the worst thing that could happen if I make the wrong decision? I would say that nine out of ten, if not more, are reversible. If I make the wrong decision, I can always change it later." She says that about one out of ten decisions may take a bit more time to think about, but with most decisions you can risk moving more quickly. "I always try to remember that if someone is bringing me a proposal or wants a change they are recommending, they have probably spent a lot of time getting to that decision. The first thing they deserve from me is attention. Otherwise, you're going to squelch people's desire to bring you ideas. There is nothing worse than working under someone who cannot make decisions, and there are a lot of people out there who are high rollers in companies that don't know how to make decisions."

At American Italian Pasta Co. (AIPC), employees know that "this is the way we've always done it" is not a good answer to give to CEO Tim Webster. "I say, we're only 12 years old, we've never *always* done anything." He shares, for the first time publicly, a classic example of facing a challenge that happened when their company began. "Borden was clearly the industry leader of pasta in 1990, when AIPC came into the business. They had over a billion pounds of North American pasta business," Webster recalled. "They were close to their customers, they were growing, they had the best factories, and they ran flat out for good costs. In our business, running flat out also equates to good quality because the machines need to be run in a consistent manner. They had a guy, John Westerford, who ran the company with an iron hand. He was the man—it was his company. He had a hunting lodge in Florida and a fishing lodge in Canada, and he had his jet flying customers back and forth all the time. They dominated the industry." The second day after Webster joined AIPC as its Chief Financial Officer, he and a team of company executives met with Westerford. The Borden executive was interested in buying a plant that AIPC owned, which was in a desirable location for Borden. Webster and his colleagues thought selling their plant might be lucrative financially. But the offer from Borden was nowhere near what AIPC had anticipated. In the midst of the negotiation, Webster recalls, "He [Waterford] looked at us, and he had these blue eyes, I'll never forget them—they were kind of going back and forth at us. He had come in on this big jet with this big fur coat and was sitting in the airport in his fur coat, and he said, 'Sell me your company or I will squash you like a bug.' It scared the hell out of me. I thought, 'Oh my God, what have I done? I've left this perfectly good CPA firm and now I've got this big nasty guy that controls this industry and he's out to get us—he's going to squash us.'

"Long story, short, he didn't squash us like a bug. That company is gone now." Webster explained that when Borden got new ownership they "booted him out because he was all omnipotent—that scared the new owners of Borden and they made him retire. The company started to fall apart right after that. But, to tie all that together to the status quo, I say over and over again to our people in every meeting, we've gone from nothing to industry leadership in a very short period of time. And ten years from now, are we going to be like Borden—on the heap, gone, and broken, or are we going to have advanced our leadership position? I think the single most dominant characteristic is going to be our attitude about how we perform. And if we don't improve tomorrow, and if we don't go at it with the same tenacity as when we didn't have any customers, and with the same starting humility we had in the beginning, then ultimately we are vulnerable. If somebody can go across the street and start a new plant, make it better quality at a lower cost with better service, then they'll have our customers. It will just be a matter of time. So I think that is what challenging the status quo is about. We've established industry leadership, but it is not a God-given right, and it won't be sustainable if we don't continue to improve our performance." In other words, Webster realizes that change is a constant, and to maximize performance and address the complexities of maintaining its lead position, the company must continually to look for new and innovative approaches to assimilate change.

With risks, come mistakes. Leaders who are willing to challenge the status quo know this and have learned to balance the threat of making mistakes with the value of learning to grow. At Hallmark Cards, Irv Hockaday says that as a company, Hallmark is constantly generating new ideas. The risk, he says, is do they go with the idea or do they ignore it? One new idea that was being explored at the time we interviewed Hockaday involves the delivery of fresh flowers. "We're testing, and will probably launch, a national/international fresh flowers business where we will deliver under the Hallmark brand—and in a Hallmark box—from the grower to the consumer's doorstep, flowers, in about 36 hours from the time they are cut," Hockaday said. "This is a huge market. I had no idea how large that market was. In this country, it is about a $17 billion market. Now, we're not going after some of that—we're going after a smaller segment. But it's a big opportunity for us. It fits perfectly with the brand. The question then becomes, how do we do that? Is this an independent, entrepreneurial effort, or do we subsume it in our large, sometimes bureaucratic environment to protect the brand and all this sort of stuff?" Hockaday says that in the past when similar ideas have been launched, they have used both approaches. "And we have lost some very bright, promising young people if we pull these things too much into the gravitational center of the card company," he admits. "So one of the things we are going to do is sit down and talk about that. We're going to say, 'All right, clearly somehow or another it was a mistake to lose these people—they were too talented, too valuable. Now, what are we going to learn about that?' It's sitting down to see if you should do some things differently." It's a perfect opportunity to learn from past mistakes and move forward with a stronger conviction.

Hockaday says that sometimes one can celebrate failure if it was a really good try. "We try different things on the Hallmark Hall of Fame shows," he said. "Sometimes they don't work." The greeting card giant recently decided to try airing a show called Flamingo Rising on one of its Sunday Hallmark Hall of Fame television specials. The show is very different from the traditional, inspiring shows that Hallmark has aired in the past. "It is a little edgier," Hockaday said. "We think and hope it will communicate to younger women than we typically gear our Hallmark Hall of Fames to. There is some risk in that because a lot of our traditional consumers are going to say, what are you doing? That's not Hallmark. It isn't x-rated, but it doesn't have a particularly happy ending and it's not Mary Poppins. Now, that may not work—we don't know." But Hockaday has decided to take the risk, and if it doesn't work, it won't be the first time. "We've had that happen before," Hockaday said. "And we've sat down together—all the people involved in selecting the script, etc., and if it doesn't work, I'm going to say I'm glad we tried it because we have to reach out there. Then the question is, okay, why was it so awful? How can we do this better next time?"

Hockaday also brings out the issue of learning from diverse thinking. He thinks getting feedback from different generations and different ethnic viewpoints is important when evaluating risks and challenging the status quo. "I think for companies that try to do things collectively or in teams, you really need to have both. If you have just a bunch of middle-aged, white, Anglo Saxon males sitting around, as we had around here for years, you're going to miss something. On the other hand, if you have just a bunch of 28-year-old, passionate entrepreneurs, they're going to get in trouble, too. Being creative in mixing and matching is helpful." Taking risks to stay abreast of the times can either lead to successful new ventures or provide important lessons to help guide future decisions. At Hallmark, managers are willing to risk and embrace these challenges of change.

LEARN FROM MISTAKES AND RISK TO GROW

At McCarthy Building Companies, Chairman Mike McCarthy believes standing by your principles is important, as is understanding that occasionally when you take risks to grow you can expect to fail. "Expectation of failure is a very valuable characteristic," McCarthy says. "We know that of the many things we start, many will not pan out. But we'll be right there with you while they don't pan out. If you will work real hard to do your best, we will see all the good things you do, and that will allow us to use you in an even more productive capacity in the next thing we give you. We have people who are going to struggle real hard personally with failure, where we think they are really growing through that opportunity. So our acceptance of failure is a characteristic of building that trust."

Bo Calbert, President of McCarthy's Southwest Division, recalled his own personal example of a time when Mike McCarthy took a big risk. "When I was just 29 years old, Mike allowed me to go do the biggest job that McCarthy had ever done. It was building the Dartmouth Mary Hitchcock Memorial Hospital in Hanover, New Hampshire. It was the largest project McCarthy had ever contracted to do, and he allowed me, as a young guy—

when there were a lot of guys much more experienced than me—to go do that. I remember a few years after the project was finished, Mike was on a trip to New Hampshire and he visited the hospital. He wrote me a note afterwards, telling me how impressed he was with what I had done up there and how I had done it at such a young age." McCarthy had watched Calbert handle some difficult field projects as a young engineer and decided to take a risk and give the young engineer a chance—it turned out to be a good risk.

McCarthy admits, however, that sometimes when he takes a risk, mistakes happen. "Usually if they are a person who has proven in a capacity before, I'll put them back in that capacity until they come to me or one of the other executives and say, I'm ready to try something new and be totally responsible for it. Once you've decided you're responsible for something, there is no place to hide. The good news, and the bad news, is we are very direct about our expectations. I try to find people that will live or die for a particular endeavor. People who will take complete accountability and will be the champion, carrying the flag for that endeavor. And then if they fail, we get them out of that and get them into something else because now they are an even richer person because they have learned how not to do things. They will be more effective in the future. Everybody needs to be needed. Everybody needs to feel worthwhile. So, even if they make a mistake, they need to understand—you made a mistake, but you are not one."

At the Ewing Marion Kauffman Foundation, Lou Smith also expects a certain number of mistakes. "You learn from them," he says. Smith recalled that early on in his tenure at the foundation, his leadership team was making a presentation to the board about some of the organization's very successful programs. "One of the board members said, 'Now tell me about the things that didn't work,'" Smith recalled. "Part of that [process] is having a leadership team or a board that says, 'Yes, we want to hear about your successes, but we also want to hear about those projects that weren't as successful as you had hoped, and that's a way to test whether you have learned anything going forward.'" Smith says creating an environment where people will be recognized and rewarded for trying something innovative and for taking risks is important, because if one project didn't work, but they learned from it, the next project may be more successful. Smith also suggests that people be cautious about how they define success. "I think perhaps the fatal blow for an organization is to believe that it is a success. I think the fatal blow for an individual is to believe, 'I am a success.' Because, guess what? Then you will stop learning. You will stop taking risks because you think you are a success. Successful individuals and successful enterprises, in my opinion, continually listen, learn, and lead. It is a never ending process."

True leaders also understand that fear and doubt are natural. Frank Hennessey asserts that the truth is, all of us have moments of doubt—when we lack self-confidence on a new initiative or a new product. "You've got to be willing to stand for what you believe in—even if it's not at the moment the most popular," says the CEO of MascoTech. "You've got to be able to show your ideas and motivate your people. You've just got to stay true to your convictions and be willing to fail. I say to people, there's no such thing as failure, there's only success and progress. You've got to be a risk taker. You can't be a leader unless you're willing to be a risk taker. You've just got to stay true to your beliefs—you have to be dependable. People have to know that they can rely on you for your support no matter what. That's what a true leader does."

Vicki Henry says that at Feedback Plus, no two clients are alike. Thus, when it comes to status quo, there is no such thing. As mystery shoppers, Henry says, "We have everything from going into a restaurant, eating a meal, and filling out a form to going into the city pound at three o'clock in the morning to pick up a car just to see how we are treated. There are no limits to what we can do. There truly is no status quo, and I believe that you either go forward or you go backward, and we don't want to go backward." Henry believes that few businesses can sustain longevity without learning to embrace change. "The fact is that some products are in demand and have a high profit spread. So if you happen to have the right product at the right time, you're going to make money off it regardless of how you operate. I think there are a lot of companies that can go into business and make money short term, but I don't know how lasting it is if you don't take care of your people and encourage them to adapt with change."

When a leader is unwilling to take risks, James Nicholson says you risk "freeze-framing" your organization. At PVS Chemicals, Nicholson encourages a certain number of mistakes, because no risk taking results in no mistakes—which leads to no growth.

True leaders understand that risk means growth and that to sustain growth in a fast-paced, ever changing global market, they must be decisive, ready to turn on a dime, and willing to take risks.

EXPLORE AND DISCOVER

- What kind of risk taker are you?

- How do you encourage others to take risks?

- What lessons have you learned from risks you have taken?

- What's the next "burning platform" to be addressed in your organization?

- How proactive are you?

- What is your greatest fear about taking risks?

- How well do you handle change?

- How resilient are you?

- How do you go about generating new ideas?

- What do you personally do to demonstrate the importance of embracing change?

11

Respect the Importance of Balance

In a business world where chaos is often considered the norm, living a balanced life may seem out of the question. Not for true leaders. True leaders know and understand that while absolute balance may not be achievable, keeping balance in mind and continually striving to achieve it are nonetheless important. "It's always been my feeling that if you don't have balance, then it affects everything—your personal life and your business life," said Gary McDaniel, CEO of Chateau Communities. "I've never really understood why people think they have to work 100 hours a week in order to have accomplished the job, because I've never felt that you do have to work 100 hours a week if you work smart—if you plan your time, if you prioritize and get things off the list. Then, on an ongoing basis, you ought to be able to have a regular work life and a regular family life." McDaniel tells his people that family should be their number one priority. "It's a heck of a lot more important to me than the job, and I think it should be more important to everybody than the job. There are a lot of organizations that expect that you give 80 to 90 hours a week to work. I think that's counterproductive." McDaniel doesn't necessarily think flextime is the answer either. He thinks that most people realize that sometimes getting the job done means taking 60 hours while another time it may take less. The main thing is making sure the job gets done. "If at three o'clock in the afternoon you think you need to leave and go do something personal, I trust in your judgment and know that you're working hard and you're not going to leave something hanging that has to get done."

McDaniel recalled that one day a man came to him, looking for a job, who had been working for a competitor. "He said that he had been working about 100 hours a week and he wanted to take off at two o'clock in the afternoon to take his son to a baseball game. His boss came in and said, 'Well, you can't do that. You've got all these other projects to complete, and everybody else is working hard around here, so you stay until five o'clock.' Well, that's ludicrous. That's the kind of thing that actually makes people want to look for a new job—which is exactly what this guy was doing. Now there may be some people that thrive on that, and there may be some organizations that work effectively because they attract those kinds of people [workaholics]. It would certainly never work for me and I could never work in an organization like that. I assume people are honest and I assume people are hardworking and are going to want to get the job done and do it well." McDaniel draws the analogy of someone who may steal from the company. "My philosophy is that you're punishing all the people that are not going to steal by putting in systems that make everyone's life more difficult because of the action of one. I've never believed in that. I don't make assumptions that everybody's a crook." Similarly, McDaniel says he doesn't assume that people won't take whatever time is needed to do their job. As long as the work gets done, he feels that there ought to be times when people leave early to attend things like their child's baseball game.

Being committed, accountable, and responsible doesn't necessarily translate to giving up the joys of personal life. Lou Smith says he loves being at the Ewing Marion Kauffman Foundation, "but my life doesn't end if I'm not here. I, and we as leaders, should not be consumed by the enterprise. We call it balancing life."

Dan Woodward learned the hard way the importance of balancing life. At age 40, as CEO at Enherent, Woodward admits that legacy has become more important to him than anything else. Balance is required to make that happen. "Up until about six months ago, I had a life expectancy of five years," Woodward shared. At age 35, Woodward allowed work to consume his life, until it nearly killed him. Challenged with making an early success out of a joint venture within the major corporation he worked for at the time, Woodward was determined to do whatever it took to make the first year a success. He did—but at a great cost. One night at the end of a year of constant travel and putting in long hours, Woodward suffered a heart attack while driving home. He's not quite sure how he made it to a hospital that was on his route home. But he did. There, he was rushed into the emergency room where doctors worked frantically to save his life. At one point, he was considered clinically dead. "To say I've been a lucky man is to put it mildly," Woodward admits. "Today, because of a set of experimental drugs, I literally have a complete functioning heart with a normal life expectancy. So I'm not going to drop dead at 45. When you're thinking about those things, you're thinking about legacy a lot." Woodward admits that balance is probably more difficult than he realizes, but today he definitely strives to have it in his life. "I work at making my time—my time with my wife, my time with my kids. The thing that I probably put aside the most historically was myself. I don't do that any longer. I've been very focused on what I do for me. I probably still don't devote as much time as I should, but I find that when I do, I'm able to do all the other things and spend the other times more effectively and feel good about it.

"I get up every morning and feel incredibly blessed. You know, when waking up is the goal, you can never have a bad day. So, if you set the bar right, how can you be unhappy? I can be dissatisfied, but I can't be unhappy. I wake up—it's a good day. Keep things in perspective. That's helped me a lot over the past five years." Woodward says that if you can't understand and empathize with people and their personal lives and what they have to deal with, "I don't think you can make balanced business decisions. You can't just go for revenue, and you can't just go for profit. You have to find balance." So, in Woodward's more balanced mode of operation, what does he want his legacy to be? "I want people to say that I allowed them the opportunity to experience being themselves, and the opportunity to do all the things that they could do—that they had an opportunity to get some personal benefit and contribute as a result—and that I had a positive impact on their lives. That's what I'd like to leave behind—that I gave people a chance and they succeeded and felt good about it and then they did it for somebody else. That's my work legacy."

Kip Tindell of The Container Store believes that people have different tolerance levels, and therefore as a leader, it is important to know individuals well enough to counsel them on what balance means to them. "But," he admits, "it is really hard to balance business and personal life when you are really committed to your business. You see it as an important aspect of your life—not just a job." Tindell says sometimes it's easy to blur the distinction if you love what you are doing enough. "The real artist of life might blur the distinction between business and personal life to the point where they are doing what they want to be doing," he says. "When Monet was out there painting, was he working or was he playing? He was doing what he wanted to do." Tindell uses himself as an example. "If you ask my parents, they'd say, 'He works too much. He shouldn't.' But this is what I want to do." Tindell admits, however, that family must always come first. "We make that very clear," he says. "Family and friends are the most important things in life, so that proves that business is tertiary [third in order], not secondary. We have a lot of women in their thirties who have children and awfully important jobs. This is retail, and retail is so diverse it traditionally takes a lot of hours to get it done. They want to be the very best they can in their careers, so you counsel and guide them." At different life stages, different choices are made about what balance is and what it is not.

Ann Hambly says balance is extremely important to priorities and the bottom line. "I try to remember that all the time," says the Managing Director of Prudential Asset Resources. "It is hard because there is so much to do here and you can get stuck working long hours. But, no matter what, you have to keep people comfortable with the fact that you put them above your job. It is a balancing act, and I think it is harder for women. This generation of women is struggling—my generation anyway." Hambly says that every day she sees women struggling between wanting to be home with their children at certain times, yet worrying that they may not be getting things done at work if they take time to be home. "My kids are grown now and I find that a much less heavy burden on me. But, for much of my career, that wasn't so. You always feel guilty—at least I did. It is very important to have that balance, and I always like my employees to feel that if they need to stay home when their kids are sick, or they have day care issues, as long as they get their job done, they are just as good to me as an employee who is here until eight o'clock every night. Staying late doesn't necessarily mean they are good employees."

Another issue of balance Hambly points out is making vacation time a priority. She recalled what her husband told her a couple of years after they got married. "He said something I will never forget. He said, 'All I am asking is two weeks of your year. You give work 351 days. I'm asking for two weeks, and in those two weeks, I don't want you calling in or doing e-mails. All I'm asking for is two weeks.' I thought, 'Wow, that is a very fair request.' So every single year, almost without fail, I take two to three weeks and we go away. I don't do phones. I don't do e-mails. I think a good leader doesn't need to be here every single day, so I can be gone three weeks and I do that. That's balance for me." Hambly says that when she returns from vacation she feels totally reenergized. "It is charging your batteries for three weeks. I feel completely renewed, refreshed, and I'm able to think things over. I am more of a thinker when I first come back. You get caught up in the day-to-day stuff so easily, and the time away gets you to think. It is very refreshing. I do much better work when I'm back. And things don't fall apart when I'm gone. My family is much better for it, I'm much better for it, my body is—gosh—it's wonderful. I highly recommend it."

When a leader fails to encourage some element of balance, the organization often incurs hidden costs from sick days, mistakes, and people being so burned out that they aren't able to give the job their very best. Gary Nelon says, "I think that if your organization is made up of imbalanced people who aren't taking good care of themselves physically, who aren't taking care of themselves spiritually, and they aren't renewing their minds constantly, trying to increase their education, then something about the overall organization is not going to be in balance." The First Texas Bancorp Chairman says he is absolutely and positively convinced that you cannot slight any one of those—mind, body, and spirit—without suffering some imbalance in the organization. "The more that you can do to nurture those three things, the better off you will be for the long term," he says.

Vicki Henry learned the importance of balance early in her entrepreneurial role. "I was a member of the CEO Institute for over ten years," said the owner of Feedback Plus. "And I saw more companies go under because of burnout than any one reason." Henry admits that it is easy to become burned out and not even know it. In a small way, it happened to her. "I can remember specifically one afternoon I was trying to put a three-ring binder together to deliver to Neiman Marcus and I couldn't get the three holes to line up. I thought, 'What's wrong with me?'" An employee pointed out what Henry herself couldn't recognize. "I can tell you right now, you're going through burnout," the employee told her. "I gave that some thought. She told me the best thing I could do is get on a beach for a week or get away and get rest." Henry took her advice. What she learned from the experience was that when the leader of the company suffers from burnout, it's easy to take all the employees down with them. "Burnout is a really critical issue," she concludes. Today, Henry offers flexible job schedules for her employees and accommodates special needs. "You can come in this office on almost any Saturday or Sunday afternoon and find people working—we've got loyal, dedicated people. But if they want to go to their son's soccer game Wednesday afternoon at three o'clock, they know that's fine. I'm a big believer that just getting the job done is what counts—not the hours in which it takes place. So we offer a fairly flexible work schedule."

Young workers entering today's workforce have already concluded that while work is important, balance is more important. Irv Hockaday sees it more and more among the ranks of young employees at Hallmark. He believes there is great value in striving for balance. "My own view is that I think people in leadership positions who have a broader, richer sense of what life is all about tend to be better motivators, communicators, advocates, and supporters. The young people I talk to want to know there is some purpose for coming to work everyday." It's an astute observation from a savvy CEO, because all research indicates that the Y generation not only expects balance in their lives, but if they don't feel they have it in one work environment, they will not hesitate to move to another where balance is valued. Balance will increasingly play an integral role in the new generation of leaders.

TOUGH BALANCING ACT

Tim Webster says he loves his family and he's going to be there for them. "But ultimately you have to fill the responsibility of your job if you want the salary and the bonus and the stock options and all the other stuff," says the CEO of American Italian Pasta. "I feel a tremendous responsibility to live up to the way I'm compensated. I believe in hard work, and I don't believe you can have everything. I don't believe you can be a great executive, a leader in the community, on the board of five companies, the soccer coach, and be involved in church and work around the house, etc., etc., etc. It's sort of the American mentality that you can have everything. I think it's dangerous. And I don't think it is realistic." Webster says that he has cognitively decided and emotionally accepted that a lot of things in his life that he used to participate in are not part of his life anymore. "There are sacrifices to be the CEO of American Italian Pasta Company and be husband and father. I don't play golf anymore. I don't play cards anymore. I went to a baseball game last night for the first time in two years, and I did it with a couple of business people." Balance requires some sacrifice.

Len Roberts conveys a similar feeling. "You can't do three things," says the Chairman and CEO of Radio Shack. "You can't succeed professionally, you can't have a good family, and you can't have a lot of personal hobbies that don't involve your family. So the problem you have is that you have to give up something. You can give up trying to climb the success ladder and have a lot of hobbies and have a good solid family. You just can't do all three. I think CEOs and leaders have a great responsibility. I can't have hobbies. I don't do things for myself. I don't go out with the guys. You've got to give something up. The bottom line is that if you work hard and you have a lot of personal hobbies, your family is subject to break and it's just not worth it." Roberts said a profound moment in his life came when his father suffered a heart attack—a moment that he uses to put striving for balance into real perspective.

Roberts said he barely had time to reach his father's bedside and spend the last few hours with him before he died. It came at a time when Roberts was going through great difficulties at Shoney's, the fast food company where he was CEO at the time. "There were big headlines in *The Wall Street Journal* [about Roberts and the difficulties], and I came to my father's death bed with that energy," Roberts said. "My father held my hand and said, 'At the end of the day—your work cycle so to speak—you're going to forget about all these things. Your mind forgets about it. And what you're going to have is the friends and family that you met along the way.' And it's so darn true!" said Roberts. "At the end of the day, that's all you have left!"

With today's technological marvels, separating work from personal life is becoming more difficult. More and more people are connected to work through palm pilots, cell phones, pagers, and a myriad of devices that allow work issues to intrude at all hours of the day and night. Yet it all comes down to personal choices and the willingness to ask the hard question that only each and everyone of us can answer for ourselves—at what cost?

True leaders understand that they have commitments to live up to and a responsibility to grow the business and generate profits. Yet, regardless of generation or gender, true leaders are also keenly aware that balance plays an integral role in achieving long-term success, and that in the long run, short-term success often comes at a very high cost.

EXPLORE AND DISCOVER

- How balanced is your life?

- How could you work smarter, rather than harder?

- In assessing your own drive for success, what is it costing you in terms of family, friends, health, and personal growth?

- What signs of burnout would you recognize?

- Do you know anyone who is at the burnout stage? Could it be you?

- How able are you to tune out work when you go home at night?

- How do you encourage balance for others that you manage or lead?

- How lenient are you about employees taking time from work for personal issues as long as their work gets done?

- How frequently do you take vacation time without checking in with the office?

- What can you do today to begin to strive for more balance in your own life?

12

So What? Predictions for the Future

In the previous chapters, we have identified ten major principles that emerged from interviews with CEOs and presidents who make a difference by building people and profits. We believe these men and women are representative of the true leaders of the future. We believe that the strategies and philosophies by which they operate will be the standards for successful organizations in the future. So what next? Based on our findings, we predict the following trends:

Valuing Values

The most effective leaders of the future will have a strong social value. In Chapter 1, we addressed four dominant values that drive true leaders: Social, Utilitarian, Individualistic, and Traditional. In past years, the Social value would rarely have shown up—

particularly among leaders in large, publicly held organizations. However, we predict a growing trend for organizations to select leaders who have a sincere desire to help people, and who will genuinely demonstrate to their employees a sense of caring and value. The Utilitarian drive must inherently be a part of any successful leader's values. Practicality demands that organizations deliver results and profits to endure. However, in a business environment where the very people that provide the work necessary to generate profits increasingly have felt undervalued, leaders who have an ability to balance an inherent caring for people with a reasonable drive for return on investment will be the long-term winners. Yes, it is important to make money. But consistency of profit will become more valuable than short-term spikes of profit.

While the Individualistic value of having the power to control one's own destiny is almost imperative to ascend to a top leadership role, we predict that true leaders of the future will clearly understand the value of submerging one's ego—or, as James Copeland so eloquently put it, they will not "breathe their own exhaust." The quest for individual power and control will be replaced by the recognition that real power and control comes from collaboration and respect for everyone's contribution. Thus, the leaders who will best serve their organizations will be driven to control the destiny of others, not just their own. We also believe that these leaders are less self-promotional and more we-oriented. Therefore, they will be less inclined to seek high visibility because their egos will not require the notoriety of some of their predecessors. When they do respond to public attention, their response will be with humility and with a strong sense of purpose.

There will be increased efforts to match values when hiring and developing leaders. The other trend that emerges from this chapter is an increased awareness of the importance of hiring people with values that are aligned with the company's values. Attitude will play a larger role in selection than aptitude. Leaders will realize that emotional intelligence is not just another gimmick, but rather an essential element for right-fit hiring. Emotional intelligence theories will be increasingly accepted as one way to measure compatible attitudes. Assessments like the TTI Personal Interests, Attitudes, and Values assessment, which we used to measure attitudes and values of our interviewees, will become as integral to the hiring process as skill-based testing and measuring behaviors—probably more so. Tricon Chairman David Novak put it very succinctly when he talked about developing leaders: "I think you can have all different styles, but you have to have unity in values."

Probe for Passion

There will be an increased demonstration of passion. In Chapter 2, we emphasized that passion is a prerequisite for true leaders. Through numerous examples, we shared the importance of passion demonstrated by the leaders interviewed. Passion is not a word that would have been used in hard-core business discussions in the past—particularly among men. Yet we predict that passion will not only become a prerequisite for leadership, but it will be more openly discussed. To attract followers, leaders must make an emotional connection. Leaders that appear aloof and superior distance themselves from people and are considered unapproachable. As the pool of talented employees narrows, leaders will find attracting the best and the brightest increasingly important. This attraction is more likely to occur when passion prevails. Additionally, people who feel the passion are more likely to replicate it, thus reinforcing throughout the organization everyone's passion for fulfilling the company's mission and purpose. With more passion comes greater authenticity. Look for both.

Seeing the Future

Visioning will become the responsibility of leaders at all levels. In Chapter 3, we explored the importance of true leaders being able to see what others may not always see. We predict that the ability to recognize opportunities and see the future will be increasingly required at every level of the organization. As organizations grow through mergers and acquisitions and reduce layers of management, having new ideas and directions emerge from all levels of the organization will become vital. As a result, leadership will need to be more discerning between strategic thinking and visionary thinking. A strategic thinker is not necessarily always visionary. A strategic thinker may have a great ability to see information from a global perspective, yet lack the ability to link the thinking to specific new products, processes, or markets. An individual with visionary thinking, however, sees the future, links the opportunity to specifics, and understands strategically what has to happen to implement the change. Matching those who think strategically with those who are visionary will become important to maximize opportunities for the future. And identifying these people at various levels within the organization will be important for optimum effect.

Communicate to Connect

Effective listening will become imperative to a leader's success. In Chapter 4, the emphasis was on communication. But the trend here is not the technological advances to aid communication or the increased ability to communicate rapidly and massively. That is reality—not a trend. The trend is enhanced listening. If you're only keeping score of your accomplishments, you don't have to listen. Today, however, keeping score is a small slice of the competitive picture. To move beyond scorekeeping, actively hearing what is really going on is imperative. The shift of attitudes predicted by the Social value—placing a higher value on caring about people—demands effective listening. To demonstrate sincerely that you care about people, both internally and externally, you must listen. Less talk, more listening. Customers and employees have heard it all. They've been misled by ad campaigns that promise more than can be delivered. They have certainly come to realize that when the sign says customer service, they are not likely to receive it. Too often, what has been communicated has not been delivered, and little evidence suggests that individual's concerns and needs have been heard. To regain trust, it is now time to stop telling and listen—truly listen. We believe that this trend is so critical that if you don't have it, it won't much matter what else you do have. Without the ability to really listen, effective learning and leading will not happen.

Leaders will set boundaries and encourage relationship building. On the technology side of communications, e-mail has run amuck. It is out of control. Rather than be optimized, it has become a shield to avoid personal interaction. And organization leaders are to blame. We predict two trends. One, leaders will accept accountability and establish boundaries for how e-mail is used. This is not a policy issue to be determined by the human resources department—it is the responsibility of the leader at the top. Two, after realistic boundaries are set on communicating via e-mail, leadership will encourage good, old-fashioned, informal, one-on-one communications to strengthen relationships between peers and colleagues. This is not a step backwards. Rather, it is a critical step forward to use both technology and human touch to maximize understanding, rapport, efficiency, and productivity.

Never Ending Learning

There will be cross-generational learning. In Chapter 5, we recommended that learning be treated like dirty dishes—never ending. The trend here deals with retirement, which is being rein-vented as we write. Sixty-five is no longer a relevant age for re-tirement. With many of the baby boom generation now in their mid-50s, the wisdoms of a vast number of workers will be lost. Thus, we predict that a shift in thinking will occur about the value that seasoned employees bring to the future of an organization. Closely tied to this trend is the issue of storytelling. Nearly every emotional tie to a company's brand—be it products or company name—is tied to a story. Take Microsoft for example. Integral to the company's identity is the story of its founder, Bill Gates, drop-ping out of college to start Microsoft. It's a story that is frequently repeated and memorably tied to the company image as it contin-ues to change and grow. Even today, Ford Motor Company con-jures up memories of young Henry Ford and his Model-T. Storytelling is an important strategy in building brand identity.

As employees have become more transient, and longevity be-comes a thing of the past, retaining corporate storytelling will be-come increasingly important to maintain company culture and values. To ensure that corporate storytellers are in place and that the legacy of leadership lives on, it will become increasingly im-portant to find ways to integrate the old with the new and to find appropriate ways to attract not only the best and the brightest of the new, younger hires, but to retain the best and the brightest of the veterans. When this happens, we predict cross-generational training. The seasoned veterans of the company will mentor younger employees with their wisdom, and the younger em-ployees will mentor older workers with their knowledge of new information and new technology. Companies that embrace this trend will have a distinct competitive advantage and will elimi-nate much repetition and reinvention.

Electronic learning will no longer be used across the board for cost-cutting purposes. E-learning and interactive learning is here to stay. But the trend is that true leaders will become more astute in the appropriate use of these technological learning tools. True leaders understand that the medium is not the most effective for many types of training. Therefore, they will make decisions less on cost effectiveness and more on learning effectiveness.

Teleporting—the next big thing. Very new in the technological trends of teleconferencing and training is a method of teleporting. This variation of utilizing hologram technology enables a presenter to appear before an audience anywhere in the world as if they were physically there. The greatest benefit of the technology is that it provides two-way, interactive communication as if the individuals were in the same room. At this time, the technology is still quite costly. We predict, however, that with increased exposure and usage, costs will come down and the technology will become an invaluable tool for simulated face-to-face meetings, conferences, and training.

Individuals will assume responsibility for managing their own career path. Another trend that involves learning is a trend towards self-responsibility and self-accountability for career management. A definite trend is emerging away from the patriarchal role of the corporation being responsible for an individual's career path. While we believe that a company's responsibility is still to provide growth opportunities through learning, we also believe that a move is on toward self-accountability—that each individual recognizes that they have the ultimate responsibility for managing their own career. The only job security is one's own ability to perform and remain an asset.

Tell the Truth

Leaders will create more opportunities to demonstrate their own accountability. In Chapter 6, we addressed the importance of honesty, integrity, and telling the truth. From a leadership perspective, accountability works best when it is modeled. So, if leaders themselves demonstrate accountability, others are more likely to demonstrate it as well. Thus, we predict that leaders will more avidly demonstrate accountability, making sure that they do what's right and tell the truth.

We also predict that successful leaders will be more truthful with Wall Street. They will work to establishing more long-term credibility with shareholders, who will be realistic enough to realize that sooner or later the truth will catch up with the companies that falsify information for spiked profits, and that in the long term, truth and consistency will pay dividends.

Building Trust

To gain and maintain credibility, leaders must increasingly demonstrate authenticity and trust. In Chapter 7, we presented the increasing importance of trust. This is a definite trend. Trust is increasingly a must.

Both employees and customers have had their trust in leaders eroded. In commercial markets, many time-honored brands can no longer be trusted. Firestone is a prime example. To counteract this, we are seeing a trend of terms such as *trust mark* and *love mark* trying to compensate for the distrust brought about by companies who have failed to live up to their brand image. Branding a product or a service is the manifestation of what a leader puts into place. We predict that leaders will be exposed increasingly to a fishbowl environment from a responsibility, accountability, and credibility standpoint. Words alone won't get it. Actions will speak louder than words. If the leader is perceived as not being trustworthy, the brand won't be trusted. The lack of trust will be reflected in reduced revenues and market share. If the company is publicly held, its stock price will plunge. Employees who lack trust in leadership will not maximize performance and will not be inspired to demonstrate passion and loyalty.

A perfect example of the short sightedness of this kind of leadership is a story that came to us from a manager within a company where the use of hundreds of trucks is critical to doing business. (The company's CEO is not among the true leaders interviewed in this book.) The managers received communication from leadership directing them to make no mechanical repairs on trucks until after the end of the quarter, so that the company could reflect good earnings for Wall Street. Not only did this directive impede the managers' ability to perform the services needed to generate income, it sent a clear message of deceit, which breeds distrust. Eventually, this cycle of distrust catches up—often with devastating long-term results. Imagine the potential impact of a major accident caused by a failure to make necessary repairs. No public relations damage control would be able to reverse the damage and restore trust.

Recognizing the Value of People

Leaders will increasingly find way to demonstrate that they value people as their greatest asset. In Chapter 8, we shared many examples of how true leaders demonstrate that they genuinely believe that people are their greatest asset and consider recognizing and building their people important. Recognizing that people really are a company's greatest asset is not a trend—it's simply a fact. Leaders who fail to see this will fail to attract the best talent. We do predict a trend, however, that more and more leaders will find unique ways of recognizing their most precious assets. Also, leaders will increasingly see the value of removing political hierarchy from the work environment and seek multi-level input to enhance innovation. We also predict that leaders will be more encouraging of entrepreneurial thinking within the corporate environment.

Increased Intuition

Leaders will increasingly give credence to the power of intuition. In Chapter 9, we address the once taboo topic of intuition. In a world where change is the status quo, having a good vision in place is not enough. Having intuition in your back pocket to help you do reality checks and course corrections is increasingly important. So we predict an increased acceptance of the power of intuition. More companies will seek training for executives to help them tap into their natural intuition, and we will see more scientific support for the validity of intuitive thinking.

Foster Risk Taking

There will be increased risk taking. In Chapter 10, we addressed the need for risk taking to more quickly capture windows of opportunity in a fast-paced world. We predict much more risk taking. In order to differentiate, especially in commodity products, delivery services, packaging, and customer service, innovation is needed. Innovation requires risk. While you don't have to be a highly innovative company to be successful, if you aren't innovative, you probably won't get noticed.

Environments will be more forgiving. If you're going to take risks and be innovative, you will make mistakes. We predict more forgiving work environments. As companies become less fear-based and more accepting of honest mistakes, employees will do more learning and growing. Punishing mistakes creates a fear-based culture, which attracts people unwilling to take risks. If you want innovation, you must expect mistakes and be willing to forgive them.

Believing in Balance

More than lip service will be given to the importance of balance. In Chapter 11, we provided some poignant examples of the importance of balance—Dan Woodward's heart attack and Len Robert's message from a dying father. We predict that leadership will increasingly accept and promote the need to strive for balance. Leaders will be less effective if they are only work focused. More and more, they will see the value of allowing their life to show through without seeing sensitivity and caring as a weakness. Gone are the days when men and women must hide their genuine feelings. Increasingly, an ability to be authentic is admired and respected. Increasingly, people who want a life will be authentic enough to get a life, and they won't be embarrassed to show it. Jack Kahl is right when he speaks about not parking your heart on the curb—the time is right for real men and women to reveal what's in their hearts as well as their heads.

Younger people entering the workforce not only expect balance, they intend to have it. Those with strong leadership potential will not tolerate a lack of understanding for the need to have some element of balance in their lives. If you can't provide it, they will find an environment that will. We predict an increase in a life-after-corporate attitude. Younger men and women are both opting for balance rather than the fast track. In corporations where this trend is not understood, talented future leaders will be lost to the competition.

Other Trends

More honest feedback will be given. We also predict an increase in rich feedback. Rich feedback provides a new kind of benchmarking, where performance standards reflect the truth about strengths and weaknesses and where honesty helps to guide people into roles they are best suited for rather than desperately trying to be what they are not. Individuals will be evaluated more fairly on the competencies required for the position rather than across-the-board skills. In the case of leadership development, more emphasis will be placed on soft skills than in the past.

Increased attention will be given to exit interviews. We additionally predict that increased attention will be given to exit interviews when someone leaves the company. This trend is tied to the listening trend. By truly listening to why people are leaving, valuable lessons can be learned and potential changes made.

The look of a leader will be dressier. We predict new guidelines for dress down. While causal dress is quite likely to remain the norm for most of the new economy companies, designer casual will become the norm for those who aspire to ascend to leadership positions.

In more traditional corporations, we predict an increased expectation of leaders to look like leaders. Retailers are already experiencing an increase in sales of tailored, sophisticated clothing for men and women. Whether openly expressed or not, a definite "look of a leader" will exist—if the look doesn't fit for you, you probably won't fit for them.

Business Structure

As organizations embrace the described trends, we also believe that a shift in thinking will take place about the people who serve on their boards of directors. We predict that forward thinking companies will attract board members who are strongly aligned with the company's core values. Boards will make clearer decisions about core issues that hold the organization true to its purpose and mission.

It was pointed out to us during our research that had JC-Penney not shifted its thinking away from its longtime value of serving the mass markets of hard working, midlevel income people in small towns and outlying rural areas, perhaps a retailer called Wal-Mart might never have become the giant retailer it is today. We found this interesting and thought provoking. When values change, it's like starting at ground zero. When values remain consistent, it becomes a matter of changing strategies and tactics to respond to changes, which is a whole lot easier and quicker.

WHAT ABOUT YOU?

The true leaders included in this book have clear and consistent values. We predict that knowing and honoring the values that are important to you will serve as the cornerstone for your own leadership development and the way you move forward in your leadership roles. Draw from the strength of your values, learn from the true leader principles and examples, and make them your own as you continue on your leadership journey.

APPENDIX A

About Students
In Free Enterprise
(SIFE)

The mission of Students In Free Enterprise (SIFE) is: *To provide college students the best opportunity to make a difference and to develop leadership, teamwork, and communication skills through learning, practicing, and teaching the principles of free enterprise.*

Founded in 1975, SIFE has become one of the world's fastest growing nonprofit collegiate organizations. Its principle is simple. Through teaching others, SIFE students gain a practical understanding of the free enterprise system. SIFE Teams, mentored by faculty advisors and the local business advisory boards, spend the academic year conducting educational outreach projects. For example, hundreds of children in California are learning how to identify and meet market needs on their way to starting their own businesses through SIFE *Youth Entrepreneurship Camps.* In Texas, *Seeds to Success,* an interactive coloring book available in both English and Spanish, teaches hundreds of elementary school students how

191

to earn money, while emphasizing personal responsibility and business ethics. In Missouri, a SIFE team created *YEA!, the Young Entrepreneurs Association* to help prepare sixth and seventh graders to be effective members of the global economy, reaching more than 6,000 students in 17 countries. Another SIFE Team program, *Cow Bank,* lends milking cows to village families in India; the families use some milk themselves and sell the rest and repay the loan with the cow's first female calf. Globally, SIFE projects have resulted in an Internet Café in Albania, economic lesson plans for deaf secondary students in Russia, and the development of a catering business in Kazakhstan, to name a few.

Each year, SIFE gives students the chance to showcase their outreach programs to business leaders and entrepreneurs at regional, national, and global competitions. Judged on how well they have taught others a working knowledge of the free enterprise system, they are rewarded with more than $400,000 annually in prize money for outstanding projects. National champion SIFE Teams win the opportunity to move on to the ultimate level of competition, the SIFE World Cup, where the world's top-rated SIFE Teams participate in one of the most prestigious and exciting events ever created for college students.

SIFE World Headquarters, located in Springfield, Missouri, provides leadership training, career opportunities, and world-class competitions, all at no fee to thousands of students each year.

SIFE operates at 1,000 colleges and universities in 25 countries, including 750 colleges in the United States—about 30 percent of all of U.S. colleges. College campuses in the United States recruit faculty advisors, called Sam M. Walton Free Enterprise Fellows. The Fellows mentor and motivate the SIFE Teams, and students develop outreach projects and literally go out into the community to teach what they have learned. "Our goal is that the students on the team have a better understanding of free enterprise, and also that everybody they reach has a better understanding," says SIFE CEO Dr. Alvin Rohrs. "SIFE Teams reach about three million school kids every year—we call it the ripple effect. They reach close to a million other university students every year. We want students to learn leadership, teamwork, and communications, and we say we do that by having students learn, practice, and teach the principles of free enterprise. We take all this head knowledge they have gotten out of the classroom, and we say, 'Now take that marketing class you just had and go out there and help that guy opening up his new café down on the corner. See if you can help him market his café better.' Suddenly, they find out there's a big difference between a business plan and what really happens. It's really kind of putting legs under everything that they are learning in the classroom."

In 2001, 750 U.S. college SIFE teams and 250 Global SIFE Teams were in places such as Africa, Australia, the Ukraine, Uzbekistan, Poland, Russia, Brazil, Albania, Tajikistan, the Philippines, South Korea, and Malaysia. SIFE students value the idea of seizing their opportunities and making a difference. Through a collaborative effort between business and education, SIFE Teams are working to improve the quality of life and the standard of living around the world by teaching the principles of market economics, business, and entrepreneurship. That's why more than 170 top corporate executives sit on the SIFE Board of Directors and provide both financial and leadership support. Inspired by the energy, passion, and healthy idealism SIFE students possess, these businesspeople and community leaders champion the ideas that hard work pays, free markets work, democracy leads to prosperity, and freedom brings social responsibility.

We were first introduced to SIFE through Manco's founder, Jack Kahl who, in turn introduced us to SIFE President and CEO, Alvin Rohrs. Rohrs invited us to attend a Board of Directors dinner in Dallas, where we heard major company executives extol the virtues of the organization and their honor to be affiliated with it. During that dinner, a young woman who was a part of the SIFE team from San Marcos College spoke. Her team had been the national winner that year in the SIFE competition. Her presentation to the group was passionate as she conveyed the tremendous personal growth she and her team members had experienced through their SIFE projects. She demonstrated incredible business acumen as she recounted the breadth of the programs the team had delivered during the year. At that moment, it was clearly evident to us that we had encountered not just another organization trying to do good, but an organization that was making a powerful difference by instilling in young people the importance to embrace free enterprise through the application of knowledge and the belief in servant leadership. We decided that very evening to donate a percentage of *True Leaders'* royalties to this meaningful and impressive organization.

Later in the year, when the national competition was held in Kansas City, Missouri, we were fortunate to have been invited to attend and to help judge. We came away from that experience being totally convinced of our right decision and with a profound respect for the entire SIFE staff and the faculty advisors who recruit and support the students, as well as the business leaders who provide valuable funding for SIFE. More importantly, we came away from the competition very proud to know that in our own small way, we will be able to play a part in helping these students and emerging true leaders to create a better and more prosperous future world.

For additional information on SIFE, visit the organization's Web site at <www.sife.org>.

Dan Woodward's Leadership Evaluation

LEADERSHIP ATTRIBUTES

Strong Personal Convictions. Leaders demonstrate strong personal convictions to a core set of beliefs and values by which they live their lives and to a select set of key issues and actions believed to be vital to the success of the unit.

Visionary. Leaders have a well-developed sense of what the future will bring, and they seek responsibility for the creation of and the commitment to a vision for the future.

Emotional Bonds. Successful leaders establish emotional bonds of trust with individuals and the team.

Inspirational. Inspirational leaders establish emotional bonds of trust with individuals and the team.

Team Oriented. Leaders recognize and demonstrate that a team can achieve more than a collection of disjointed individuals can.

Risk Taker. Leaders understand that gain can only be achieved with a commensurate level of necessary risk.

Drive to Excel. Leaders constantly seek to improve themselves, their team, and Enherent.

LEADERSHIP BEHAVIOR
(O=Behavior Evident 100%, M= Behavior Evident Most Times, B=Focus Areas)

Strong Personal Convictions   RATING

Earns respect from others for high consistency between
attitude and behaviors.   _____

Keeps commitments and promises.   _____

Leads by setting a good example.   _____

Makes honesty a high priority in all circumstances.   _____

Demonstrates commitment to Enherent's values.   _____

Honors issues that pertain to fairness in the workplace. _____

Exemplifies leadership guided by strong personal values
and solid integrity.   _____

Visionary   RATING

Uses innovative thinking to solve complex problems.   _____

Maintains an appropriate balance between addressing
business and interpersonal issues.   _____

Continues to seek and to learn new information that may
help Enherent.   _____

Promotes productive debate and discussion.   _____

Constructively challenges the current state of affairs by
championing new initiatives for improvement.   _____

Actively searches for promising opportunities to expand
Enherent's business.   _____

Exemplifies leadership based on intelligent, visionary
thinking.   _____

Emotional Bonds   RATING

Establishes loyal and enduring relationships.   _____

Shows a strong desire to discuss the views and opinions
of others.   _____

Expresses own opinions with perspective and emotional
maturity.   _____

Demonstrates a positive and constructive outlook.   _____

Refuses to manipulate situations to secure personal
success above all else.   _____

Builds relationships based on mutual respect.   _____

Exemplifies the ability to build good working relationships
that are based on emotional maturity.   _____

Inspirational   RATING

Inspires people to excel.   _____

Demonstrates an ability to build positive excitement in
the organization.   _____

Acts on constructive feedback.   _____

Inspires people to care about their work.   _____

Calls attention to improved performance with recognition
or rewards.   _____

Uses communication skills to motivate people.   _____

Exemplifies the ideal model of an inspirational leader.   _____

Team Oriented   RATING

Publicly rewards the team based on the success of its
combined efforts.   _____

Leverages the dissimilar skills and styles of diverse work
teams to achieve superior results.   _____

Reaches an effective balance between retaining and
delegating authority.   _____

Promotes productive cooperation between groups
within Enherent.   _____

Works to foster a sense of mutual accountability among
team members.   _____

Assigns diversity a very high priority on the team.   _____

Exemplifies what it means to use effective leadership
skills to promote good teamwork.   _____

Risk Taker   RATING

Faces difficult situations with courage and persistence. _____

Has the confidence to make sound decisions even in adverse
circumstances.   _____

Accepts the negative consequences of risk taking graciously
and confidently.   _____

Demonstrates the confidence to defend a justifiable but
unpopular decision.   _____

Takes risks by trying out new ideas, approaches, or methods. _____

Welcomes exploration by championing new ideas and
encouraging others do the same.   _____

Exemplifies leadership that is guided by confident and
constructive risk taking.   _____

Drive to Excel   RATING

Seems to thrive in high stress situations.   _____

Delights in rising to the challenges of the future. _____

Shows a strong interest in improving performance beyond
the minimal acceptable level. _____

Is driven to move information quickly and accurately within
the organization. _____

Pushes projects to achieve results that are beyond
expectations. _____

Works with a well-paced, energetic drive. _____

Exemplifies the ideal model of a leader who is motivated
to excel. _____

TD Industries's One-with-One Discussion Card

When TD Industries supervisors meet one-with-one with employees, both employees and supervisors are given the following card to help make the conversation meaningful.

To: _____

Your One-with-One is scheduled for _____

_____

A One-with-One is intended to help keep communication lines open between you and your supervisor.

Once a year, you and your supervisor should meet at a time convenient to you both. Although the meeting can be at your job site or in your office, there should be some privacy so that you both feel free to talk openly.

We hope your One-with-One will help you and your supervisor better understand each other's job and that you will more clearly see your job as a part of the whole.

On the other side are questions for you and your supervisor.

Among the questions you should ask your supervisor are:

1. What do you as my supervisor consider my strong points?
2. What do you as my supervisor consider my weak points?
3. How can I be a more effective member of your team?

Your supervisor, among other things, should ask you:

1. What do I do, and what does TD do, that helps you most in your job?
2. What do I do, and what does TD do, that hinders you most in your job?
3. What can I do that will help you do the best job for TD?

The Average True Leaders Attitudes and Values Graph

The Attitudes Graph displayed here represents an Average True Leaders Attitudes and Values Graph as determined by averaging the numbers from the 27 individuals interviewed for this book. If you would like to take your own Personal Interests, Attitudes, and Values assessment to see how you measure up against the True Leaders in this book, go to <www .true-leaders.com> for information and directions.

The Personal Interests, Attitudes, and Values assessment is a copyright product of TTI Performance Systems and is distributed by The Price Group, a certified TTI partner distributor. Bette Price, President of The Price Group, is a Certified Professional Values Analyst and a Certified Professional Behavioral Analyst.

TTI is the world leader in computerized behavior (disc), attitude assessments, and soft skills. TTI products are proven, research-based solutions, designed to assist with the challenges of employee performance, selection, and satisfaction. TTI's world headquarters are located in Scottsdale, Arizona.

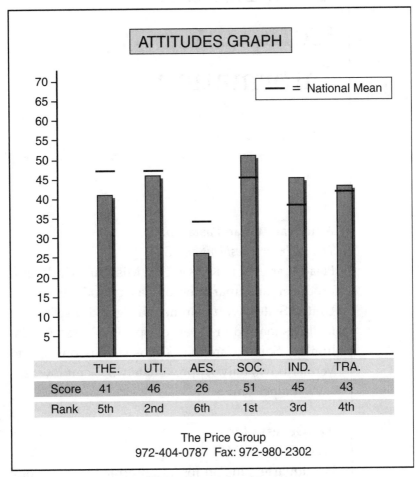

ATTITUDES GRAPH

	THE.	UTI.	AES.	SOC.	IND.	TRA.
Score	41	46	26	51	45	43
Rank	5th	2nd	6th	1st	3rd	4th

The Price Group
972-404-0787 Fax: 972-980-2302

True Leaders Company Information

American Italian Pasta Co.
Tim Webster, President and CEO
Headquartered in Kansas City, Missouri. The largest producer and marketer of pasta products in the United States, with manufacturing and distribution facilities located in Excelsior Springs, Missouri; Columbia, South Carolina; Kenosha, Wisconsin; and Verolanuova, Italy. Approximately 550 employees.
<www.aipc.com>

AppGenesys Inc.
Bruce Simpson, CEO
Headquarters in San Jose, California. A technology company that helps manage Web application infrastructures through staging, testing, tuning, deploying, monitoring, and scaling services.

BHE Environmental, Inc.
John Bruck, Chairman and President
Headquarters in Cincinnati, Ohio, with branch offices in Ohio, Tennessee, Texas, Missouri, Pennsylvania, and field offices in California. A privately held company that provides a full range of professional environmental and remediation services to industrial, commercial, and governmental clients.
<www.bheenv.com>

Chateau Communities
Gary McDaniel, CEO
Headquarters in Greenwood Village, Colorado, with operations in 34 states. The largest self-administered and self-managed real estate investment trust (REIT) in the United States specializes in the long-term ownership, management, acquisition, and development of manufactured home communities.
<www.chateaucomm.com>

The Container Store
Garrett Boone, Chairman and Cofounder; Kip Tindell, President, CEO and Cofounder
Home office is located in Dallas, Texas. A store devoted to "helping people streamline and simplify their lives by offering an exceptional mix of storage and organization products." Approximately 2,000 employees nationwide.
<www.containerstore.com>

Deloitte & Touche
James Copeland, Jr., CEO
More than 100 offices in over 100 U.S. cities. A leading accounting, tax, and consulting firm. Over 30,000 U.S. employees

enherent Corp.

Dan Woodward, Chairman and CEO

Headquarters in Dallas, Texas, with locations in Connecticut, New York, and Barbados. From IT architecture and design to implementation and ongoing support, *enherent* creates solutions that work and customer relationships that last. *enherent* provides ebusiness answers for a variety of companies—from the Fortune 1000 companies to emerging dot-coms. Clients include industry leaders in financial services, banking and capital markets, insurance, pharmaceuticals, health care, high-tech, hospitality, and travel and tourism.
<www.enherent.com>

The Ewing Marion Kauffman Foundation

Lou Smith, President and CEO

Located in Kansas City, Missouri. A private foundation that works toward the vision of self-sufficient people in healthy communities. Grantmaking partnerships in support of youth development and activities designed to accelerate entrepreneurship through the Kauffman Center for Entrepreneurial Leadership.
<www.emkf.org>

Feedback Plus, Inc.

Vicki Henry, CEO

Headquarters in Dallas, Texas. A privately held marketing research firm that provides customized research programs for companies seeking to evaluate the interaction of their employees with customers. Twenty-six full time employees and a database of over a hundred thousand preshoppers nationwide.
<www.gofeedback.com>

First Texas Bancorp, Inc.

Gary Nelson, Chairman and CEO

Main lobby in Killeen, Texas, with locations in Copperas Cove, Round Rock, Georgetown, and Belton. A bank offering "a full range of services including commercial and real estate lending, deposit services, cash management, and ACH processing." <www.firsttexasbank.com>

General Accounting Office
David Walker, Comptroller General
Headquartered in Washington, D.C., with other offices throughout the country. The investigative arm of Congress. GAO exists to support the Congress in meeting its Constitutional responsibilities and to help improve the performance and accountability of the federal government for the American people. GAO examines the use of public funds, evaluates federal programs and activities, and provides analyses, options, recommendations, and other assistance to help the Congress make effective oversight, policy, and funding decisions. In this context, GAO works to continuously improve the economy, efficiency, and effectiveness of the federal government through financial audits, program reviews and evaluations, analyses, legal opinions, investigations, and other services. GAO's activities are designed to ensure the executive branch's accountability to the Congress under the Constitution and the government's accountability to the American people. <www.gao.gov>

Hallmark Cards, Inc.
Irv Hockaday, President and CEO
Headquarters in Kansas City, Missouri, with locations worldwide. The personal expression industry leader, and virtually synonymous with consumers' preferred brand of greeting card. "When you care enough to send the very best." <www.hallmark.com>

Manco, Inc.
Jack Kahl, Founder
Headquarters in Avon, Ohio, with products available at hardware and other stores across the country. A Henkel Group company

that develops and markets a full line of innovative home, office, and do-it-yourself products.
<www.manco.com>

MascoTech
Frank Hennessey, CEO
Headquarters in Taylor, Michigan. A diversified industrial products company with world-leading metal forming process capabilities and proprietary product positions serving transportation and industrial markets. Annual sales of $1.7 billion with over 60 manufacturing locations and 9,500 employees. (MascoTech was acquired by Heartland Industrial Partners, a private firm, in late 2000.)
<www.mascotech.com>

McCarthy Building Companies, Inc.
Mike McCarthy, Chairman
Headquarters in St. Louis, Missouri, with locations in Dallas, Phoenix, Las Vegas, Newport Beach, San Francisco, Sacramento, Portland, and Seattle. Oldest and largest privately-owned construction firm in the United States, ranked among the top 10 U.S. general builders and the top 100 global construction firms. Approximately 2,500 employees.
<www.mccarthy.com>

Plante & Moran, LLP
Bill Matthews, Managing Partner
15 offices located throughout Michigan and Ohio. Ninth largest certified public account and management consulting firm in the nation, providing accounting, tax, consulting, and financial planning services to businesses, government, not-for-profit, and health care organizations and individuals.
<www.plante-moran.com>

Prudential Asset Resources
Ann Hambly, Managing Director
Headquarters in Dallas, Texas. A leading commercial mortgage servicing business, with the capability to tailor services to fit the needs of clients and a customercentric philosophy that creates value for borrowers and investors alike.
<www.prudential.com>

PVS Chemicals, Inc.
James B. Nicholson, President and CEO
Headquarters in Detroit, Michigan, with locations in New York, Ohio, Illinois, Indiana, Georgia, Ontario, Canada, Mexico, and Thailand. A chemical production company, specializing in sulfuric acid, sulfur-based products, ferric chloride, environmental waste treatment, hydrochloric acid, full-line chemical distribution, and aluminum chloride.
<www.pvschemicals.com>

Radio Shack Corporation
Len Roberts, Chairman and CEO
Headquarters in Fort Worth, Texas, with locations nationwide. Primarily engages in the retail sale of consumer electronics through the RadioShack store chain. As of December 31, 2000, RadioShack operated 5,109 company-owned stores located throughout the United States. Approximately 25,000 employees.
<www.radioshackcorporation.com>

Sleep America
Debbie Gaby, President; Len Gaby, CEO
Headquarters in Phoenix, Arizona. More than a dozen stores in the Phoenix and Tucson, Arizona, metropolitan areas. A mattress retail store whose goal is "to make mattress purchasing a convenient and enjoyable experience for Arizona residents."

Students In Free Enterprise

Dr. Alvin Rohrs, CEO

Headquarters in Springfield, Missouri, with offices worldwide. The world's preeminent collegiate free enterprise organization. SIFE provides leadership training, regional expositions, and career opportunity fairs for thousands of college students throughout 20 countries, and awards more than $400,000 in prize money to college student teams each year.

<www.sife.org>

TD Industries

Jack Lowe, CEO

Headquarters in Dallas, Texas, with office locations in Atlanta, Austin, Houston, San Antonio, and Washington, D.C. The premier construction and service company, providing mechanical, refrigeration, electrical, plumbing, building controls, and energy services to customers in Texas and throughout the Southwest for over 50 years. 1,400 employees (now called *partners*).

<www.tdindustries.com>

Terri's New and Consigned Furnishings

Terri Bowersock, Founder

Headquarters in Phoenix, Arizona, with locations in Arizona, Georgia, California, Colorado, and Nevada. The largest consignment furniture chain in the country; helping clients sell their used furniture through the consignment process. Seventeen national locations.

<www.consignanddesign.com>

Tricon Global Restaurants, Inc.

David Novak, Chairman and CEO

KFC is based in Louisville, Kentucky. TRICON Global Restaurants is a quick service restaurant (QSR) company with more than 30,400 units in over 100 countries and territories. The four operating companies are Kentucky Fried Chicken (KFC), Pizza Hut,

Taco Bell, and TRICON Restaurants International. Through its concepts, TRICON develops, operates, franchises, and licenses a system of both traditional and nontraditional QSR restaurants.
<www.triconglobal.com>

Weight Watchers, International, Inc.

Linda Huett, President and CEO

Headquarters in Woodbury, New York, with offices worldwide. A leading weight management program that operates through group meetings and a simple system for monitoring food intake and calculating its nutritional value.

INDEX

l

ABOUT THE AUTHORS

BETTE PRICE

Bette Price is an author, consultant, and professional speaker who, since 1982, has been President and CEO of The Price Group, an organization dedicated to assessing and developing strategic planning, leadership, and performance issues. Her clients range from small to mid-sized businesses to major corporations in such diverse fields as technology, engineering, environmental, professional services, and health care. For the past ten years she has been affiliated with TTI Performance Systems, Ltd., in Scottsdale, Arizona, and by using their assessment tools has become certified in the science of measuring why and how individuals perform. Price has worked with such major corporations as IBM Global Services, Alcatel, Sony Electronics, Smurfit-Stone Waste Reduction Services, and JCPenney Corporate Headquarters.

As a consultant, Price challenges the status quo to ignite new ways of thinking. As a business keynote speaker she brings real life experience to the platform when she speaks on the topics of leadership and market development.

Price is a former award-winning television and newspaper journalist who has hosted her own television shows in two major markets and was a columnist and feature writer for the *Kansas City Star*. She was a part of the team coverage that earned the newspaper a Pulitzer Prize for its coverage of the tragic Hyatt Hotel skywalk collapse. Price is an active member of the National Speakers Association (NSA), having received the organization's President's Award for distinguished service in 1993. She is currently Chair of NSA's Editorial Advisory Board and the Consultant Professional Expertise Group. Price is a member of the Institute of Management Consultants (IMC), a member of the Board of Directors of the Dallas Chapter, and Chair of its Practice Development Committee. She can be reached by email at bette@pricegroupleadership.com.

GEORGE RITCHESKE

George Ritcheske is an organizational effectiveness consultant, executive coach, and speaker. He began his career in Human Resources in Detroit with Coopers & Lybrand, after earning his BA in Economics at Dartmouth College, where he played varsity football, and an MBA at the University of Michigan. As a group, and then Regional HR Director, he functioned as an internal consultant to business unit leaders in Michigan, Ohio, Indiana, and Kentucky. In 1989, he moved to Dallas and spent four years immersed in merger integration with Deloitte & Touche. The challenge and stimulation of interacting with groups to create better ways of working together led him to establish his own business, HR Partners.

In 1999, George formed an alliance with CoachWorks and split his business into two parts. CoachWorks Leadership Group encompasses the leadership team effectiveness consulting and executive coaching lines of business, while HR Partners continues to provide customized training design services and expert facilitation of people development workshops. As a professional speaker and seminar leader, George has addressed such topics as The Transformational Leader; The Challenge of Change; Team Building for the 21st Century; The Manager as Teacher, Leader, Coach; and Leading Your Own Development.

George is committed to helping leaders and leadership teams to develop into leaders that people want to follow. He resides in Coppell, Texas, with his wife of 26 years, Bobbi. They are the proud parents of 21-year-old twins, John and Kate. He can be reached by e-mail at george@coachworks.com.

True Leaders

For special discounts on 20 or more copies of *True Leaders*, please call Dearborn Trade Special Sales at 800-621-9621, extension 4307.

Dearborn™
Trade Publishing
A **Kaplan Professional** Company